From stars to wild
lilacs + all the
joy in between —

Diana Coogle

An Explosion of Stars

Diana Coogle

Laughing Dog Press
Blue Ridge, Georgia

These essays were first broadcast
on Jefferson Public Radio, Ashland, Oregon.
The following were also printed in the *Jefferson Monthly*:
"Meeting the Earth Goddess," "The Enchanted Forest While It's Still
Enchanted," "Disappearing Frogs," "An Explosion of Stars," "The Dump,
the Landfill, and the Transfer Station."

Copyright 2004, Diana Coogle
Printed in the United States of America
Library of Congress Control Number: 2004097924
ISBN: 0-9669364-2-6

Laughing Dog Press
Blue Ridge, Georgia 30513
*

P.O. Box 3314
Applegate, OR 97530
dcoogle@roguecc.edu

This book was set in Times New Roman, 12 point.

For all my friends mentioned herein,
especially Maren, Louann, Ela, and Leah

Contents

Acknowledgments

With enormous thanks...

To Tom Nash of Southern Oregon University for his impeccable editorial eye, witheringly accurate red pen, deep knowledge of the English language, unstinting encouragement, and brilliant sparks of inspiration. The arguments were fun.

To my son, Ela, over-busy with his own career as a sculptor, musician, and performer, yet immediately generous with his time and expertise in designing the cover. I am grateful for his computer skill, the standards of excellence that made him turn down all my suggestions till we found the right answer, the time he gave to this project, and, most of all, his constant and loving support for what I do.

To my sister Sharon, who with her own sharp eye for language and graphics and a piercing intelligence, caught a lot of goofs I'm glad have been deleted. She lent her talent to the text, cover design, and page layout, talked me through a lot of problems, then said, "What else can I do to help?"

To Liam Moriarty of Jefferson Public Radio and Lucy Edwards, formerly of JPR, who produced these and many other of my essays as commentaries during my two decades of broadcasting. They are both outstanding radio producers.

To Sharon Coogle and Joan Peterson for proofreading, though all remaining errors, of course, are my responsibility.

To Kim Ball, as always, for QuarkXpress help and to Rocky Hayes for last-minute computer assistance.

To all the people, anonymous and known, who participated in my titles poll.

To Chuck Crandall and the other folks at ADR Bookprint for being great people to work with and doing outstanding work.

It is the telling that is the charm, for it is the expression that gives to our imaginations the experience of the tale. And that, surely, is the singular gift of every good book: the scenes and moments – the "fancy pictures," as Hawthorne calls them – that with their prolonged and indelible coloration convey again the joy and anguish of distant landscapes.

– Mary Oliver

Introduction

Just after I fell asleep in my tent on top of a pass in the Oregon Cascades, the wind started snarling over the mountain. With startling ferocity, its rough hands began throttling the neck of my tent, threatening to dash the tent – with me in it – off the mountain. Rain thrashed and pummeled. Lightning zapped its eerie light. Inside the tent I cowered.

The storm raged all night. Even after I knew the tent was secure and I was safe, I sat upright in my sleeping bag for hours, tense and alert. It was a long night, the night of my 60th birthday. Inevitably, perhaps, my thoughts turned to those past six decades. I considered my childhood in rural Georgia: my four siblings who were also my playmates, my good parents, the family dog Rusty, my cat Pokey, the horse we kept one summer named Patches. I thought about those wonderful years when I was a Marshall Scholar at Cambridge University: my boy friend, who was blind; my tutor, Sita Narasimhan, from India; the passion for literature I was following then and have never relinquished. I thought about the wild hippie years that succeeded Cambridge; the years of building my little mountain house in nature, where I still live; the years of raising my son, Ela, who, having just been my hero in a windstorm, was braving the rest of the night with Leah, his wife, in their own tent. Story after story came to mind as though I were a storm-tossed Sheherazade crunching 1001 nights into one, holding back the sword of the storm with the wonder of words. I fell asleep before my 1001 stories were told, but not before I had conceived of this book.

That night the stories arose in no seeming order, but any good Freudian would say the order was following its own unsuspected logic. The essays in this book also have a possibly subconscious relationship in their sequencing. The collection begins with a walk on the mountain through clouds of wild lilacs and ends with my sweeping the sky with binoculars to find the "explosion of stars" of the book's title. My intent is that the essays support and enhance the ideas, themes, and tones of each other, but to follow the sequential logic might be a sort of Nabokovian game, fun but unnecessary. The stories can be read in any order. Each was originally broadcast on Jefferson Public Radio and so was written as an independent essay. Each was meant to be a gem on its own.

An Explosion of Stars is about places I've been and people I love. It's about my passion for literature and art, for the earth and the stars, for flowers and frogs, for language and music. It's a book full of family, friends, and foibles, stories that entertained me for hours while the wind raged against my tent in the dark of the night. Maybe for that reason a wind of passion swirls around the essays, giving each its particular glow and gently urging the reader into the next.

Diana Coogle
Applegate, Oregon
November 2004

An Explosion of Stars

An Explosion of Stars

Wild Lilac Walk

Because the morning is refreshingly cloudy and cool after our weeks of beastly hot weather, I've decided to take one of my favorite cold-weather walks. The trail leads through an almost-old-growth forest onto an old logging road heading up the mountain where walking under the sun is warm and pleasant on a winter day but too sweaty and hot to be nice in the summer – except in the cool of dawn, but a recent cougar sighting has kept me from walking at that time of day. It might be a good walk this overcast June morning.

The woods are tenebrous and cool. There is little green in a forest like this, where the understory is open ground and the overstory a woven tangle of unseen branches. On a sunny day, that warp and woof break the sunlight into mottled patterns on the forest floor, but today the space between the big trunks is dusky and even. What matters here is not color but texture. Stippled, striped and cross-banded with lines of grey, ridged and grooved and rutted, cracked and ribbed – in places indented, nicked, nocked, and reticulated – the trunks call attention to surfaces. Every once in a while a smooth madrone, rising out of a thick, dark, shaggy base, snakes through the rough, straight trunks of the firs. If I'm close enough, I'll pass my hand over the muscular limb or scoop up a handful of crinkling, papery, sloughed outer bark. I touch the scabrous, wide limbs of an old oak on the trail. Corrugated trunks of incense cedars loom here and there, and through the woods I catch sight of the jigsaw-puzzle bark of a Ponderosa pine. I step over a cedar log that has rotted to its dusty innards, as flaky as a French croissant.

As I break out of the forest onto the open road, the world changes. All at once I am walking up the mountain through an avenue of wild lilacs, bright with subdued sunlight. As far as I can see, clouds of pastel blues, purples, and whites hover on both sides of the gravel road. The road itself is covered with a mass of bright yellow creeping bird's foot, the air subtly perfumed with wild lilac sweetness. Textures are no longer rough and hard but fluffy and lacy. I pass between long branches of feathery blossoms draped over the upper cliff on one side and, on the other, cirrocumulus bushes of heavenly blue fringing the dark forest that slopes downhill. The road is my boat through a sea of color – lilacs of periwinkle blue next to alabaster and pearl; powder blue between bushes of deep lavender and light orchid; light amethyst pushing into moonstone blue. I pass now a wild rose bush lifting pale pink blossoms against the delicate blues, now a patch of daisies that whitens the roadside. At the top of the cliff, in front of the lilacs at wood's edge, I snatch a glimpse of fire-engine-red Indian paintbrush. At the foot of the lilacs in another spot, I find a flurry of pink dog bane. And still, up and up, wild lilacs line the road, now framing a view of Grayback Mountain or a glimpse of the valley, now forming a spumescent foreground to the vertical lines of the forest, the way waves topped with foam give contrasting context to a fleet of sailboats. As if color attracts color, a splash of brilliant yellow flashes past me, stops in a manzanita bush between lilacs, and coalesces into a western tanager, goldenrod yellow against the green manzanita and the periwinkle, pearl, and purple lilacs. As though intoxicated by the perfume, birds sing. By all the witness of my senses, I am walking through heaven.

It's not every day we are privileged to walk through heaven, but unless I'm mistaken, I can do it again tomorrow and the next day and the next. Heaven is not forever, but until the sun burns too hot or the lilacs fade, I think I'll take a little share every morning.

Unknowable Music

I spent several weeks in Sweden the summer before my parents' 60th wedding anniversary. Because Sweden is renowned for its beautiful glassware, I thought a piece of Swedish glass would be an appropriately special gift for my parents, so I bought two crystal wineglasses from Orefors, one of Sweden's best glass makers. The crystal was as thin as a page of the Bible. Embedded in the stem of each goblet was a long dangle of thick, dark blue glass. When I flicked my finger against the rim of the crystal, a ringing tone with the clarity of a brilliantly starry winter night sang out, and, indeed, when, after my parents had opened and admired their gifts, my father stood up from his chair and his beautiful crystal wineglass fell to the floor and broke into hundreds of sharp, tiny pieces, it gave off an unforgettably beautiful, tinkling ring, as though glittering stars were falling through the heavens. The sound was so unexpectedly beautiful I hardly registered that the glass had broken, but my father was so appalled I don't think he even noticed the music.

I was in Sweden again the following summer and returned to the store to replace my father's gift. I found the same thin crystal glass with the dark blue inset. I was tempted to drop the glass on the floor to make sure it held the same music as the first one, but I just had to trust that the same crystal would have the same untappable beauty of song locked safely within the thin brilliance of glass.

A couple of days later I went with some friends to a spring in Denmark called Store Blaakilde, Big Blue Spring. Though the spring is usually tinted a deep turquoise blue, on that day the sky was covered with clouds, and the water was not blue but clear. It was so perfectly transparent it was as though it were not there. It distorted nothing through its glass, neither the swaying strands of grasses underwater at the banks nor the bottom of the pool where I could see the chalk-white, blue-tinged floor bubbling as though boiling. But this spring was boiling cold, not hot. It was ice-cold, crystal-cold, star-crystal cold. Swimming across the spring with a dozen or more breast strokes, I felt the cold hammer against the back of my neck, but instead of getting out on the far side, I turned to swim back across. This time I stopped in the middle of the pool, treading water, watching the white bubbling earth under my dangling feet. There was no estimating the depth. The bottom looked only a couple of feet below me but could have been another ten. I was looking into and through something more clear than the crystal wine glass, more sharp than air, more transparent than ice. Inside that water must surely be a beautiful music, which, like that of the wine glass, could only be known by shattering the clarity. I longed to hear it, but just as my father's wine glass, the new one well packaged in my suitcase, was more beautiful with its shape unshattered and its song unheard, so was this glittering water best kept with its song unknown. There are some beauties so fragile we must leave them intact, even at the cost of never knowing them.

France via Books

Last week I went to a book sale at the Rogue Community College library. There I found a dozen little paperback books in French that made me catch my breath. These were the same *Classique Larousse* editions I had used as a student in Aix-en-Provence in 1964. Their bright purple covers, each with its white square for the title and author's name, were swathed in a smoke of nostalgia. I picked up Jean-Jacques Rousseau's *La Nouvelle Héloise* and opened it. Like a genie kept in a bottle for 30 years and now set free, the life I had once lived swirled around me.

As I turned the pages, I heard the Mistral rustling through the sycamore trees along the Cours Mirabeau. I heard the water of the big fountain at the end of the Cours, spilling from tier to tier, and, at the outdoor cafés lining the sidewalks, a subdued chatter accented by tiny espresso cups settling into saucers. I turned a page and saw myself sitting in one of those sidewalk cafes with my French Algerian boyfriend, Paul, and his *pied noir* friends. I turned a page and was in Cézanne's studio, gazing over his easel at Mont Sainte Victoire. I turned another page and was sorrowfully telling Mme. Herbeau that the directors of Vanderbilt University's Vanderbilt-in-France program were moving me to another house – Mme. Sévin's – because they objected to my having to bathe at the communal baths down the street.

When I lifted the book to my nose, I smelled, in the old paper, the musty stink of socks from the ground floor of the movie theatre in Aix and saw myself in the balcony watching *Un Homme et une Femme*, *Jules et Jim*, and the American Westerns my French friends loved. The smell of the book was close and warm, like the sun at Les Calancs on the Mediterranean, where I sunned on white-sand beaches in my first bikini, like the hot yeasty smell sifting through open windows of cellar bakeries as

I walked to early classes, like the steaming cup of *café au lait* Mme. Sévin gave me every morning for breakfast. The smell had something of a bare wooden floor in it, too, the old-house smell of my room at Mme. Sévin's, where I studied at a tiny plank table and where Gunilla, my Swedish roommate, would lull us both to sleep in our narrow beds by speaking Swedish, "the most beautiful language in the world," she told me.

As I touched the slick, brittle paper, I was not turning pages but walking down a Provençal road, reaching to pick cherries dangling from overhanging branches, the sky so blue above the cherries and the wall over which they hung so white (and I so young) that I thought, suddenly, "Even if I were in prison, no one could take this happiness from me."

I turned a page and read, "*J'ai longtemps hésité `a te faire cette confidence*," but the words were mere sounds, the unintelligible flow of indistinguishable words of my first days in France. Then I turned the page again, and they flowed into the music of a beautiful language I once lived with and made my own.

I bought *La Nouvelle Héloise*, not to read it but because it is a genie's bottle. To unstop the bottle and let the treasures tumble out, all I have to do is pick up the book and turn its pages.

The Literary Legacy of My Father

That I am a bibliophile can hardly be blamed entirely on my father, but bookworms have their beginnings somewhere, and I suspect that mine hover around him, since it was he who read picture-books to my sister and me at bedtime and who told us stories, his own stories about the adventures of Unimac the Eskimo. Unimac performed marvelous feats in Alaska and the Yukon. In one story he was playing football and pretended to throw the ball to another player but actually kept it himself, hid it in his arms, and ran for the touchdown. I was mightily impressed with Unimac's cleverness.

The bedroom wasn't the only setting for stories. In the otherwise little-used living room was the Red Chair, a large, overstuffed throne perfect for reading. In it I could curl up with my toes tucked under my legs, sprawl with my legs hanging over the arms, and arrange myself in any number of comfortable and unorthodox reading positions. It was the only thing that made the living room lived in. That's where I suffered through the Civil War with Scarlet O'Hara, where I mourned Beth's fatal illness with Jo, and where my father sat on occasional evenings with his two or three or four or five children snuggled in his lap, propped over the back of the chair, or perched on its arms as we all lost ourselves together in the book he was reading aloud: *A Christmas Carol*, *Black Beauty*, *The Call of the Wild*.

My father was the first to give me Shakespeare. From time to time some bit of dinnertime conversation would trigger a long-since-memorized rendition of "To be or not to be" or the closing speech of *The Taming of the Shrew*. He also gave me poetry with sonorous recitations of "The Raven" by Edgar Allen Poe. The laughter in his eyes never belied the ominous tones and mysteriously ambiguous chorus line, "Quoth the raven, Nevermore." I couldn't help but thrill to the words, though the elusive meaning of the poem seemed always to hover above them, never settle into them. Again and again I listened to the magic of the mood of rhythm and rhyme as my father lamented long the lost Lenore.

"The Cremation of Sam MacGee" was a different delight, with its thrill of the frozen wasteland where a dead man would dance in glee on his funeral pyre to be warm at last. "The Cremation of Sam MacGee," Jack London, Unimac – a theme of the northlands seems to have run through my father's choice of literature, and if I had been smart enough then, I might have foreseen that he would take his family – all seven of us – to Alaska for adventure.

One other literarily relevant incident frequently occurred in our household. The family would be sitting around the dinner table, and someone would, unfortunately, ask a question. My father, who perhaps by design sat closest to the bookshelf, had only to tilt his chair slightly backward to reach the appropriate volume of the encyclopedia and bring it forward. We would groan; he would read, and I thought then and still think encyclopedias the most boring of all reading material. Nonetheless, I am my father's daughter, and the scourge of the encyclopedic lecture has been unconsciously inherited. Once when my son was very young, he said to me, "Mother, without making a big deal about it, what is five plus three?" Yes, I, too, love the northlands. I, too, read to my son. I, too, seize any excuse to teach. I am my father's daughter.

Stitching Together the Generations

"The lore of sports," says Scott Russell Sanders, "may be all that some fathers have to pass down to their sons in place of lore about hunting animals...or placating the gods." But the lore of sewing has been passed from mother to daughter unchanged. For centuries, all women learned to sew. Native American women sewed with bones and sinew. Penelope wove while Ulysses sailed. Medieval court women made tapestries and embroideries. Later, of course, men took over the commercial jobs, leaving the spinning to women, the spinsters.

Sewing is no longer a necessary personal skill, and when I was a child, I squirmed impatiently under my mother's tutelage. "Some day you'll thank me for this," she told me, but I was a child, and "some day" was too far in the future for me to care about. Ignoring my restlessness, my mother taught me to thread a needle, a skill demanding even better hand-eye coordination than that needed for catching a ball. Such a tiny eye in that needle! Such wiggly thread! Mimicking my mother and grandmother, I licked my thread and tried to shove it through the needle. "I can't get it threaded," I complained, exasperated, wanting to go outside and play.

My tutors took a look and laughed a grown-up laugh. "The thread's so wet it's limp," my grandmother said to my mother, expertly wiping the thread dry, relicking it, and sticking its stiff end through the needle. As I rethreaded my needle, I tried to imagine a camel going through that eye, and I thanked God I wasn't rich.

My grandmother taught me how to stretch a cloth on the bias to make the selvages match, how to stick pins twice through the fabric so they wouldn't fall out, and how to iron seams with my fingers, so I could sew well when I traveled.

Last Christmas while I was visiting my parents, my mother and I sorted through a drawer of fabric scraps, among which my mother pulled out a tablecloth my grandmother had been embroidering before senility set in. The embroidery was a simple outline stitch in brown thread over a stenciled design of leaves and vines. It was neither my style nor my color, but I took great joy in picking up the thread of my grandmother's embroidery where she had set it down. I delighted in carrying on with the same stitch she had begun, one thread sewing the years together. Later that day my niece asked me to help her with a Christmas-gift embroidery set. As I explained the stitches to her and we sat on the couch sewing together, I felt that thread taken up beyond me, too, now, as my niece sewed me into the future.

Scott Russell Sanders talks about the "dialogue carried on with muscle and bone" of the game of catch, but there are two dialogues of sewing. One is the private dialogue of craftswoman with craft, the needle and thread weaving a communication between sewer and cloth. The other dialogue is the ancient one among women sewing together. The slow rhythm of the needle, the monotonous repetition of in and out, opens the mind while it pulls the cloth into shape, and words flow. Secrets are shared; hearts are opened. Gossip flies. While the father is outside throwing that ball to the son, each intent on the dialogue between muscle and bone, the women are in the bedroom where the sewing machine is, pushing the bone of the needle through the muscle of the cloth and joining their hearts with the dialogue of their voices. The lore of men may have changed – no longer how to shoot a buffalo, now how to shoot a lay-up, as Sanders says – but this lore of women, this drawing of the thread through the cloth, joins us in dialogue with Eleanor of Aquitane and Murasaki of *The Tale of Genji* as well as with our grandmothers and nieces. Though my mother never explained the linguistic mystery of the eye of a needle to me, I know now what that eye sees: centuries of women bound by the thread they draw through the cloth, women's fingers stitching together the generations.

Southern Education

The eight sisters in a play called *The Octette Bridge Club* meet twice a month during the 1930s and '40s to play bridge. One year when I played the role of Alice in a community theater production, I was astounded to discover that, out of the eight-woman cast and three-woman crew, I alone knew how to play bridge.

My father taught me to play, telling me, "It's part of your education." There, in one succinct phrase, is the flavor of the culture I grew up in, that lingering aristocratic feeling of the Old South, that Faulknerian gentility of Miss Rosa and my Aunt Zilpah, a style of living already growing quaint and old-fashioned in the rest of the country.

Along with bridge, I learned to dance, but while elsewhere Elvis Presley was causing riots with his pelvic twist, creating a dance with sex, exhorting teens to shake, rattle, and roll, my friends and I were learning the waltz and the fox trot, the cha-cha-cha and the rhumba. I was in a seventh-grade cotillion club. The girls wore long ruffled ball gowns and received obligatory corsages from their reluctant and uncomfortable escorts. Carnations were pretty, but orchids carried more prestige. Although at home we listened to "Rock Around the Clock" and "Don't Be Cruel," the chaperones of our cotillion balls provided us with the Big Band sound.

Divorce was unheard-of, nudity a sin, and sex unmentionable. The scandal of my high school days was the Baptist preacher's daughter who, in real-life depiction of Flannery O'Connor fiction, ran off with a laborer working on the road in front of her house. While my contemporaries in New York City and Cincinnati were seeing psychiatrists to analyze Freudian dreams and straighten out kinky libidos, I was naively innocent of what my date meant when he called the gear shift between the bucket seats of his new car "birth control."

I went to college in the South, but from there a bigger world beckoned. While at Cambridge University in England, I became friends with Yoko Gibo, a Japanese anthropology student. Dressing me in her Japanese kimonos and accompanying undergarments, she also taught me to walk like a Japanese girl. (In England she had learned to walk like a Western woman.) Her parents expected to arrange a marriage for her, but she had learned more than anthropology in England, just as I had learned more than literature, and she wanted to choose her own mate. She was in the yawning gap between two cultures, between two eras of Japan, just as I stretched between two eras in the South.

Cotillion balls? Bridge a part of one's education? To think, had such an upbringing continued, I might have become a genteel old maid of the Old South, playing cards under the magnolias, sipping mint juleps on the verandah. Well, thank goodness for changes, both in me and in the South. But thank goodness for education, too. Someone had to teach the Octette Bridge Club how to play bridge. And if I didn't end up the Old Maid of the Old South, I'll bet Yoko didn't accept an arranged marriage, either.

Sita, in Saris and Sweaters

Sita Narasimhan, an Indian immigrant to England and a fellow at Newnham College, Cambridge, was my tutor in Elizabethan literature while I was at Newnham as a Marshall Scholar in the late '60s. She wore her thick black hair in one long braid down her back and had the Hindi's red dot in her forehead. Her eyelids were so beautifully darkened that I understood why women use eye shadow. She wore beautiful silk saris, but, like most Indians in England, she suffered from cold, so she always wore a heavy wool sweater, too, counteracting the sensuous effect of the sari.

She held weekly tutorials in her flat, where the gas space heaters were always on, whatever the weather. Each week I would park my bicycle at the gate, both dreading and excited by the coming session. Sita would invite me in, gesture to a comfortable chair before the gas heater, and offer me a glass of sherry. Too shy to be at ease, awed by the sherry and by Sita's grace and graciousness, I would mumble thanks and wait.

Sita would settle comfortably in a chair next to mine. Then the torturous part of the tutorial would begin. In her rich, deep, rough voice with its singsong Indian accent, Sita would ask me, "What do you make of the Red Cross Knight's sojourn in the House of Pride in Canto IV of Spenser's *Faerie Queene*? Why does Prince Arthur appear in Canto VII? What is the symbolic significance of Duessa's red clothes?" I would stumble through answers, tongue-tied not because I hadn't studied but because what I had to say was so inadequate next to Sita's wisdom. Finally Sita would take pity on me and start talking herself – so eloquently, with so much understanding! I sat like a disciple at the feet of a master, bathing in her wisdom.

By my second year at Cambridge, Sita had cut her hair in a short bob and no longer wore the red mark on her forehead, though she still wore saris and still overheated her rooms. My last day in Cambridge before I left for the States, she treated me and my boyfriend, Peter, to dinner at an Indian restaurant that she chose and where she did the ordering. It was one of the best meals of my life.

After I left England, I wrote Sita from time to time, but she wasn't writing back, and we lost touch. I never forgot her, though, and when I was pregnant, I was going to call my child Sita if it were a girl.

One day I answered the ring of the telephone to hear a woman's thick, rich, deep voice with a singsong accent. "Diana," she said. "Do you know who this is?" It was Sita. She was in San Francisco for a conference. I held the receiver like a butterfly's cocoon – something precious and fragile that held great beauty – while we talked. I was so honored that she had called. I never heard from Sita Narasimhan again, but that one telephone call was confirmation enough that I had not been forgotten by the woman I always said was the wisest woman I had ever known.

Reweaving Bloom's Day in Dublin

The second year I was at Cambridge University, where I earned my masters in English literature, I dated a graduate student at Queens College named Peter, who was blind and who had gotten his undergraduate degree in English literature in New Zealand. Bibliophiles both, we decided that for spring vacation we would make a pilgrimage to Dublin to retrace, as much as possible, the route of Leopold Bloom on the famous day's journey of June 16, 1904, known ever after as Bloom's Day and rendered in literature as James Joyce's novel *Ulysses*.

We started where the novel opened, at the unused Martello tower, a large, square stone belvedere with a crenelated top and tiny slots of windows, the place where Stephen Dedalus lived with his friend and fellow student, Buck Mulligan. We climbed the "dark, winding stairs" to stand in Stephen's own room. We sat on the edge of the gunrest, like Stephen, watching a ghostly Buck Mulligan prop his mirror on the parapet. We leaned over that parapet and looked down on Dublin Bay, as Stephen had done, half expecting to see again the mailboat clearing the harbor mouth of Kingstown.

We walked the beach with Stephen, who, with his eyes closed, tapping his ash sword before him, explored "the ineluctable modality of the audible" by experiencing the darkness of the blind. Peter, blind, had no need to pretend, but I closed my eyes, like Stephen, and, because it is what Stephen heard, listened to "his boots crush crackling wrack and shells."

We found Davy Byrne's public house, where Leopold Bloom had taken a sandwich and a glass of burgundy. A tiny sign over the bar verified this as the right pub. We ordered an ale, and then, when the pub's patrons learned I was American and because this was 1967, we had to endure a rousing rendition of the "John Kennedy Ballad."

We walked through the red light district where Leopold, paternally protective, followed Stephen into his carousing, but it was no longer a brothel district, and as we walked down the street, flocks of children followed us. I was talking into a tape recorder, describing to Peter everything we were seeing. The children, fascinated, frolicked around us like large lambs. The bells of All Hallows Church, where Bloom, earlier in the day, had sat for a few minutes in the hopes of hearing some music, pealed over the street.

Finally, like Leopold Bloom with Stephen Dedalus in tow, Peter and I headed for Bloom's home on Eccles Street at the end of the day (ours ending earlier than Bloom's). It was an ordinary street of semidetached houses in the British style, all brick, each with its mortared arch over the doorway, its two front windows, its iron picket fence along the street, and its sunken basement. But at Bloom's house, #7 Eccles Street, all the illusions came tumbling down. The windows were broken and boarded; the doorway was shielded with a piece of corrugated tin. The second story was gone. Molly and Leopold Bloom had moved away some time in the 63 years since June 16, 1904, and now the house was being demolished. However, we could still see the basement windows from which Bloom had looked up at the street as he ate kidneys for breakfast. And behind those boarded-up front windows we could hear the ghostly voice of Molly Bloom in her bedroom giving the world her famous soliloquy. "... [A]nd then I asked him with my eyes to ask again yes," she is saying, "and then he asked me would I yes to say yes my mountain flower and first I put my arms around him yes and drew him down to me ... and yes I said yes I will Yes."

The Sand-Buried Church

One summer, on a bicycle excursion through the northern tip of Denmark, my friend Maren and I made a side trip to the famous sand-buried church. Two thousand years ago the shifting seas in this part of the country created a new land, a long, thin peninsula of sand dunes, eventually called Skagen (pronounced approximately *Skane*). Soon enough, of course, the Danes began inhabiting this peninsula, and by the 14th century, the people of Skagen had built a church on the dunes just within sight of the ocean. It was a typical 14th-century church with a lead roof, arched windows, and a bell tower at one end of a long apse. The sides of the bell tower had crowstep gables, notched steeply to the peak of the roof in the Danish fashion. Like most Medieval churches, the entire building was brightly painted, presenting a noble sight for the fishermen and farmers and their families as they traveled across the dunes to church on Sunday: that red, blue, and gold church standing like the bulwark of God himself, promising joy and happiness in the life to come and comfort and solace for today.

But as the centuries passed, the "ever-whirling wheel/Of change," left its mark. The winds blew, and the seas pounded at the shores, and the dunes, bereft of vegetation by grazing cattle, shifted and changed. In 1539 the king of Denmark pronounced the peninsula a protected area, prohibiting the grazing of cattle, and the farmers moved away. But still the fishermen and their families attended the proud, beautiful church across the dunes.

The sands wouldn't stay still. They continued to lay siege to the church. In the 1700s severe sandstorms hit the area. The congregation began to carry shovels with them to Sunday worship. One storm in 1775 so buried the church that the parishioners had to dig through the sand to open the doors for prayer service. By the end of the century the sands had won the battle, and the church was abandoned. Now the villagers, who were used to gathering supplies from ships stranded off their shores, began to pillage the church for much-needed building material, salvaging bricks from the walls and lead from the roof. And the sand continued with its work until it had completely buried the church and might have buried the bell tower, too, except that the tree plantations established in the 1800s as windbreaks had given the heather and grasses a chance to gain a foothold, seemingly stopping the migrations of the sands. Now visitors walk over a church they would never know was buried underfoot except for the bell tower, with its crowstep gables and whitewashed sides, looking oddly disproportionate without its accompanying church and rising from the sand like a double tribute: to the sand that moves and the trees that stop it.

But that second tribute is an illusion. To look over the sand dunes and sparse grasses, the hills and dips, the patches of forest, and the ocean in the distance, I might have thought the landscape changeless, but given the next storm, who knows where it might move? Today the trees have calmed the raging sands, but, still, if the 18th-century storms were to be repeated, who knows but that the sand might not bury the trees themselves? If a church, why not a forest? If peninsulas can rise and churches be buried, there can be no comfort and solace in our illusion of permanence.

Clock Time

When I was five, my father promised me a Mickey Mouse watch if I didn't cry when I had my tonsils out. Keeping time was a Mickey Mouse matter at the age of five, but when I was in college, time was more serious, and in my Christmas stocking I found a pretty wrist watch, the implication being that I would never lose time now that I carried all the time in the world with me on my arm.

Then there came a time when I had neither watch nor clock, when no timepiece ticked off hours and minutes, when the turn of the sun told the hours for me and the waxing and waning of the moon the months. Sometimes I lost days, but the months turned into seasons, and time was measured as it was needed. Then, emerging, I began to need a method of breaking the day more exactly into hours and even the hours into minutes. For my birthday my father gave me a digital watch.

Those who had kept their watches all along, who, keeping pace with the world, had moved faster and faster, had learned already to niche their hours more and more precisely into minutes and even into seconds. Time used to be kept in generalities with right-brain vagueness: "I'll be there around quarter till." Now the precision is crisp: "Be there at 10:43." As watches now remind us of the passing of time in seconds or even hundredths of seconds in soundless flashes on our wrists, we'll soon have to make appointments for 10:43:13. For left-brain implements, the old watches had a certain poetry about them: they had faces and hands, and they allowed us to keep our time, time, time – if keep it we must – in a sort of Runic rhyme. Digital watches demand our time, time, time in a steady, undeniable, rhythmic, robotic beat.

Time is a continuum, its parts so small they can't be separately identified. But today computers work at speeds measured in milliseconds, nanoseconds, and picoseconds – respectively, millionths, billionths, and trillionths of a second. In quantum electrodynamics, a strong force interaction takes place in a measured 10 to the 23rd of a second, with 22 zeroes between the decimal and the one. In a world in which scientists can divide the continuum of time into picoseconds and less and in which even we keep track of fleeing seconds as well as minutes, hours, days, weeks, months, and years, in a world in which seconds as well as atoms can be split, how can we not expect to see a like splitting of knowledge into nano- and pico- fields of expertise, a splitting of families, a schizophrenic splitting of personalities?

Oh, well, *tempus fugit*, whether you hear it tick away or see it flash away – or don't watch it at all. I have long since abandoned my timekeeping arm pieces. Such measurement of time is arbitrary and fabricated anyway, a convenience we have agreed to abide by. But I also agree with Faulkner that it's good to forget that arrangement from time to time: "Time is dead as long as it is being clicked off by little wheels," he said. "Only when the clock stops does time come to life."

The Ineluctable New Light of Spring

When the light returns, when the days grow longer and the night withdraws like a melting snowman, everything in nature seems to waken. The trees shake themselves and lift their heads. Even before their leaves emerge, even before the buds become blossoms, we can tell the trees have been roused from sleep. To look closely at an alder, an ash, or a cottonwood in early March is to see a naked-limbed winter tree, but to see the same trees in a grove from a distance is to discern a delicate wash of light green so subtle under the predominate red-brown fuzz of swelling buds that it strains credulity to think it's there. Flowers that have slept wrapped in their bulbs for months pop up to see what the light has brought, rubbing sleep from their eyes before turning their faces to the increasing sun. Insects stir one by one, and birds quicken with the light, singing at dawn and signing the air with curlicues and swooping flourishes like a calligrapher drunk with joy.

Here on the mountain things sleep longer than they do in the valley. Two weeks before my daffodils smile at the sun, I see the same variety massed deeply yellow in Joan's garden. While my plum tree is no more than a ruddy suggestion of the later pale pink explosion, in Jacksonville pink and white fruit trees already add a pastel frill to the streets and yards. This seasonal difference is not a function of light but of altitude. I have the same number of hours of daylight as anyone else in my latitude, the same increasing number of minutes day by day until at last we think not of day as a crack of light between the dark but of night as a blink of the shutter before the next day photo. This process begins on winter solstice, of course, but at such a minuscule pace we bank more on faith than on observation that the light will return. Then, so gradually we can't see it coming, the pace increases until, just anterior to the spring equinox, the ball of light is rolling so fast we cannot but get swept in its path. Like the rest of nature, our spirits lift as though from sleep.

And then, once awake, we have to prove to the cosmos we weren't sleeping on the job, so we tinker with the clock as though with time itself. By now daylight saving time, or the reversal of it, is so ordinary I can't remember which is the real time and which the manipulated. Some people despise daylight saving time, calling it unnatural. But clock-keeping itself isn't natural. Shifting the clock at our will is only a pretense at control. Adding an hour of light to the evening necessarily adds an hour of dark to the morning, and, in real terms, nothing has changed. As Ursula LeGuin said in a poetic variation of a truth of physics, "To light a candle is to cast a shadow." Whether you like the autumn version of the manipulated clock or the spring version depends on who you are and what you do. In the fall, school children don't have to wait for the bus in the dark, but my neighbor looks forward to the spring-ahead day so she can feed her horses in the daylight again. I myself have no preference and have a hard time keeping track of when I'm supposed to change my clock. The light comes as it comes, whatever I do to the clock, and with the coming of the light, I feel an awakening, a resurrection. Like pagans of old, like daffodils, I turn my face to the sun and worship.

Nevada Breath

I wasn't even one day away from home when the world went strange on me, and Nevada with one big suck stole my breath, carried it right over that wide plateau to the end of the planet where the curve begins, where the hills barely cling to the surface of the earth and *2001: An Odyssey* becomes reality. My breath was stretched so thin out of my body it sailed into the hazy maybe of the planet where mountain and sky and plateau blend and sweep into space, and I began to gasp, "My God! My God! It's Narnia coming!"

The unfathomable past surged as present as the surrealist future hovered real. Here where the naked land lay as rawly formed as the day it was born, the centuries of recorded history receded by tens, fifties, hundreds, till 3000 years had faded – past the ranchers who came and the two or three who stayed; past the ghostly breath of once nearby Ward, Nevada, where 30,000 inhabitants thrived (painted ladies dancing, the old upright piano tinkling, miners laying silver on tables for whisky, gamblers expending fortunes with the flick of an ace); past the Pony Express pounding the hard earth of the sagebrush basins into their distant and yet again distant ranges; past the Shoshone whose home these hills once were; 3000 years back to 1000 BC and a single man wielding a sharp implement against a sandstone cliff. Here, safe from that far edge of the chosen and given world where Narnia gave promise to a 20th-century woman, this man with his sharp implement squeezed himself into the steep chimney of a pink-flaming rock in the sandpaper cliffs of Nevada's plains. In the crack of that chimney he breathed the thick sagebrush sweetness of Nevada's breath, raised his arm and his sharp implement, and from his world framed by the width of the V in which he was wedged, incised and pecked his poetry.

Was he a madman, these lines the unearthly scribblings of madness? Or a wrongdoer, perhaps, jailed behind the stone-barred wideness of the V, procrastinating the next moment of doing nothing by scratching in the rock? Was he a shaman whose incised incantations made magic for the buffalo hunt? Was he a woman, maybe, illustrating stories for her children in the long summer twilights before bedtime? Whatever else, this hieroglyphicist was an artist, with a skill so refined the chiseled story I was now reading had retained a vigor great enough to shift time within place, to disfocus history into blurry waves, closing the gap between centuries and bringing me face to face with the now of the past.

But I am ignorant. I stumble at the foreign language, the rich symbols reduced by my ignorance to meaningless lines. Hooves here, maybe – snake, home, hunter, maybe – with large ovals and horn-like points to mean buffalo and wavy lines to indicate woman, wife, maybe, and vertical lines meaning what? I can feel the buffalo thunder across the plains. I can hear the fire snap in the cave behind me and smell the meat cooking. I breathe the same sagebrush sweetness that artist breathed. Nothing in the landscape 360 degrees around me indicates the roll of time. The silence is so deep it encompasses thousands, millions of years and hundreds of miles of distances where only God sits and listens, where only God, now, reads this story in the rocks and laughs or weeps or smiles at what it tells.

Nevada breathes hot against my legs. Unencompassable Nevada. I draw a deep breath and retreat from the V, vacating the skin of the artist or madman who wrote these stories on these rocks, incomprehensible etchings that have left, for mc, only one clear message: "Aslan was here."

Equinox at Towhead Lake

As soon as Louise and I arrived at Towhead Lake, I took a swim in its spring-fed, autumn-cold waters. Later, when the sun cast the shadow of Kangaroo Mountain over our camp, we clambered up the side of Kangaroo to sit in lingering sunshine on sand-red boulders and gaze over the dark forested ridges of the Siskiyous. When the sun started fading over the ridge, we scrambled down again, staying just ahead of its warmth, to sit in the last of its light at the lake, Louise on sun-warmed rocks overlooking Hello Lake far below, I in a crotch of the gnarled Jeffrey pine tree above her. Red Butte towered over us, its rounded top glowing red in the sunset. From the tree, I could see the afternoon blue of the sky through long, thin, green pine needles shimmering silver in the sunlight. The stillness around us was enhanced by the mysterious howling of the wind at Hello Lake, and in that stillness and from the tree, I began reciting Wordsworth:

> It is a beauteous evening, calm and free,
> The holy time is quiet as a Nun.

The fiery glow on Red Butte and the great silence absorbed the words:

> Breathless with adoration; the broad sun
> Is sinking down in its tranquillity.

Rays of brilliant light streamed from the sinking sun like mermaids' hair, striking Red Butte and hanging there so long the sun seemed stuck in its descent, as though time had been suspended to give the sun a lingering glory before winter's dark set in.

That night, before the full moon of September struck through the window of the tent with razor sharpness, I followed its rise by the dazzling white radiance sliding down Kangaroo Mountain. When I got up in the night and startled two deer grazing in the moonlight, I could see them bounding away as clearly as I could hear the hollow thump of their feet striking the earth.

The next morning I swam again. Then Louise and I struck camp to take a day hike on the Pacific Crest Trail. With our packs on our backs, we turned to say farewell to Towhead. Charmed anew by its beauty, I said softly, "It seems a shame to leave."

"Yes," Louise agreed.

We looked at each other. Louise voiced our common thought: "We don't have to leave now."

So we took off our packs and stayed a while longer. Louise tucked herself into a nook of red boulders on Kangaroo while I reclined on the large flat rocks at the lake's edge. As I watched newts squiggle through the water, flashing their orange bellies, to nip at air, words from Thoreau rose like newts to my lips: "We need the tonic of wildness.... We can never have enough of Nature" and then the beautiful wisdom of Thomas Berry: "If we have a wonderful sense of the Divine, it is because we live amid such awesome magnificence.... If we have powers of the imagination, these are activated by the magic display of color and sound such as we observe in the trees and bushes and flowers, the waters and the wind."

But the moon would be waning that night already and daylight shortened day by day from now till mid-December. It was time to take our renewed sense of the Divine into the other world with us, so we shouldered our packs again and headed out of the wilderness.

Long Lost Cousin

A few weeks ago a woman overheard me talking to the clerk in the Northwest Nature Shop in Ashland. Recognizing my voice, she stopped me as I turned to go. "Are you Diana Coogle?" she asked. I acknowledged the truth, and she went on to say how much she enjoyed my commentaries and my book, blah, blah, blah, and then said, "I've always wanted to ask you something. I have some cousins in the South named Coogle. You're from Georgia, aren't you?"

I was immediately suspicious. People are always asking if I'm related to this Kougal or that one, always spelled differently. In Grants Pass I'm so often asked if I'm related to the Mr. Cougle who teaches high school that I hope people are forever asking him if he's related to that woman who does commentaries on Jefferson Public Radio. I asked this woman how her relatives spell their name, ready to say, "No, my name is spelled C-O-O-G-L-E" and go on my way.

"Oh, just like yours," she said. "My cousins' names are Dennis and Barbara."

I could have fallen over. "But Dennis and Barbara are my cousins!" I cried, a bit offended that she had claimed my cousins. I had a momentary confusion that she was wrong, that if they were my cousins, how could they be hers when I didn't know her? It took us only a few minutes to figure it out. Her mother's sister, Margaret, married my father's brother, my Uncle Barney, who was also her Uncle Barney. Her Aunt Margaret was my Aunt Margaret, and Barbara and Dennis, Margaret and Barney's children, were cousins to us both.

"Then we must be related!" I cried. I wasn't sure that was true, but we hugged warmly, like long-lost cousins.

We chatted a bit about our mutual relations. I hadn't heard from Barbara since we were children and had last seen

Dennis at my parents' 50th wedding anniversary 13 years ago, so Lyndi brought me more up to date. I started to tell her that Donna and Marge, children of Joe Coogle, Barney's brother, were in Florida and Colorado respectively and did she know that Donna had recently divorced, but I remembered just in time that her Aunt Margaret and Uncle Barney being my Aunt Margaret and Uncle Barney didn't make all my cousins her cousins.

Someone has determined that each of us is only seven steps removed from knowing everyone else. Here seemed to be the proof. Lyndi and I had met as strangers and had parted as relations. As I walked down the street, I wondered how many of the people I passed were, by some tenuous thread, related to me. If I started a conversation with the person next to me on an airplane, would we discover that somebody in his family was related to somebody in my family? The likelihood of discovering these unknown relations seems so minuscule I marvel that it actually happened to me. But that such a discovery is unlikely doesn't negate the amazing possibility of relationships, and it underscores the importance of being kind to whomever we meet. After all, that stranger might be one of the family.

Friendly Family Competition

While I was in Georgia for the holidays, my father, my son, my nephew, and I took advantage of the mild and balmy weather for a competition in horseshoes and quoits in the back woods – Dad and Darryl on quoits, Ela and I on horseshoes. The winners of those games would play each other in quoits, the more difficult game, and the losers would play horseshoes.

Ela beat me in horseshoes; Dad beat Darryl in quoits. As we took a breather before the next games, Ela asked Dad what the quoits were made of.

"They're brass," Dad said. "They're a copy of quoits made in my grandfather's brass foundry."

I was immediately interested. "Where are those quoits?" I asked.

"One of them was lost and never found," he said. "The other three are in the basement. The dinner bell on the hickory tree also came from my grandfather's foundry."

For years my mother had rung that bell to call her family to dinner – Dad from his woodworking in the basement, the kids from their games in the woods. I had always liked it. Knowing its origin gave it extra value, and I asked Dad if he would leave it to me in his will.

"You can get in line for it," he answered dryly.

"It's grown into the tree by now," Ela said. "I know because I tried to ring it."

"Barney found that bell in a garage sale one day," Dad told us. Barney was his older brother. "He bought it without knowing it came from Granddaddy's foundry. Then one day he looked inside the bell and found 'Fowler's Foundry' engraved on it. Now that and the quoits are the only things we have from my mother's father's brass foundry."

Then we got back to the games. Ela beat Dad in quoits. Then Ela and Dad watched Darryl and me finish a close game of horseshoes. I won. We all looked at each other with great satisfaction. Three of us had won a game, but I had won by such a small margin, all four of us felt like winners. For games of competition, these had had a satisfying outcome.

"I wonder how much these weigh," Ela said, hefting a quoit.

"Oh, about a pound and a half," Darryl guessed, and we were launched on a new competition. Dad and I each picked up a quoit, too, and weighted it in our hands against an imaginary counterweight. (Mine was a pound of flour.) Then each of us having made a definitive guess, we all trooped to the basement and crowded around Dad's winemaking scales as he weighed a quoit: 18 ounces. I was the winner.

It was growing chilly, so we moved inside, where Dad suggested a game of anagrams. We played with fierce competition, making no special allowance in case Dad's mind, at his nonagenarian age, might not be as agile as it once was. Words were made and lost at a rapid rate as we challenged unknown words and shamelessly captured words from each other. *Cat* became *cast* became *tacks* became *stacks*. *Ire* was transformed into *rite*, *rite* revamped as *tiered*, *tiered* reclothed as *retired*, and *retired* finally swallowed by the triumphant *reiterated*. At the end of the game, when the letters were all used, we each had five words in front of us. We beamed at one another in mutual satisfaction.

There had been no family stories to go with the anagrams, but that game, like the quoits and horseshoes, had left a legacy of family, anyway. Even if I don't get the bell (and I hope I do) or the three quoits, I've inherited a memory of the camaraderie that day of competition brought to three generations of family.

From the Model T to the WWW

My father's 90th birthday party wasn't a gathering of a few family members in a nursing home. That's not my father! – or my mother, who had planned a monstrous four-stage party: gift-giving at lunch, dinner for 50 friends and family, a champagne toast party, and breakfast the next day. It was at the dinner party, as I examined photographs, newspaper articles, a scroll of historical and personal events, and the table decorations about my father, that I found I was reviewing 90 years of a century as well as 90 years of a life.

On the "transportations" table sat two models of my father's cars – his first, a Model T Ford, and his current, a LeBaron convertible. These two cars indicated an evolutionary leap in ease and speed of personal transportation. The same evolution in public transportation was also suggested: from propeller airplanes – there was a photo of my father standing next to his plane in his pilot's goggles – to Boeing jets, symbolized by souvenirs from New Zealand, Brazil, Soviet Georgia, and Korea, places my parents had visited in the last two decades. The 49-star flag from the family's 1959 car trek to Alaska, lying next to memorabilia from those trips abroad 20 years later, indicated an increase in leisure time, as well as cheaper and more accessible foreign travel.

The sports and hobbies tables showed no such world changes. If my father was Kentucky State diving champion in 1932 and '33, someone else holds that title now. A twin to his 1940 tarpon contest fishing trophy sits on someone else's shelf today. The ice skating, bowling, running, badminton, quoits, and tennis artifacts may look old-fashioned, but the games are as relevant now as ever. People still read. They still play the saxophone for personal enjoyment. They play cards, and if Boggle is a more modern game, nonetheless, there have always been games. The woodworking display symbolized not only my father's lifelong interest but an ancient craft, and if wine making is a development of Ken Coogle's later life, the art itself is far from modern. The tumbling display of earmolds not only represented the years my father devoted to his business but also the importance of small business in mid-century America.

Only four houses depict the permanent homes of my father. America has become more mobile since he was a young man, and I am in a minority in that my parents still live in the house of my childhood.

Late in the evening of the third stage of my father's party (champagne toasts at my parents' neighbors' house), Dad climbed the stairs to the den to view on a computer the Web page my nephew Brian had given him for his birthday. Dad sat in front of the computer as Brian instructed him: "Put your pointer here. Now click. Now click here" until my father was looking at himself on the Web: "Ken Coogle's 90th Birthday Party."

"Now click here," Brian instructed, and pictures of the family, in color, appeared on the screen. My father was a quick learner. Ninety years had done nothing to diminish his intellect. I watched his smile as he clicked and read about himself, clicked again and looked at his own picture on the computer monitor. I could tell he was pleased. And for good reason. What a day it had been! For that matter what a life it had been, and what a century. As I watched my father in front of the computer, the enormity of the span of the century compressed before me into this image: this one man, who had once owned a new Model T Ford, now surfing through his own page on the World Wide Web.

Roses, but No Chopin

At the opening of an art exhibit in the countryside around Skørping, Denmark, I met Teddy Teirup, the pianist touted as Denmark's greatest interpreter of Chopin. Not too far into our conversation, after learning that I am a writer, he suggested we make a trade: his CD for my book. We exchanged addresses, and when I returned home, I dutifully sent him a copy of my book, then waited eagerly for his CD. It didn't come, and it didn't come. Finally, a year later, I was in Skørping again, visiting my friend Kirsten, who had introduced us.

"You know," I mentioned casually one day, "Teddy never sent me his CD in exchange for my book."

Kirsten, an energetic person who wastes little time, said, "We'll just go get it, then." She picked up the telephone, dialed Teddy's number, and said, "Hello, Teddy. Diana's in town."

"Oh, Diana Coogle," he said at once. "I'm so embarrassed."

Kirsten said, "Maybe we could come over to pick up the CD now."

"Oh, yes, of course," Teddy said. "Just give me an hour to clean the house."

He lived in a long, narrow, mid-19th-century white stucco house with two little blue doors and blue shutters. He warned us to watch our heads in the doorway, a caution well in order for tall Kirsten and for him – a big, sloppy man with a worn face and a shock of iron-grey hair – though unnecessary for me. In the vestibule he gave me a big hug, saying, "My conscience is black."

I said, "Never mind. Your negligence has meant I'm here now."

Inside the house, I found myself in a long, narrow, low-ceilinged room with two grand pianos side by side, a Steinway and a Bechman. Behind them was a vaguely Romanish statue of a female figure on a small table in front of a large blue Nordic abstract painting that took up most of the wall. On a small table between the two piano benches was a vase of red roses. On top of a small organ were bottles of Chivas Regal and other alcohols. All the doors and windows were open to air the room of cigar smoke. Teddy offered port, and we sat at the dining table to talk.

Teddy was a wonderful talker. He told us about a concert composed, conducted, and organized by a Polish immigrant to Denmark. It took place in an old castle in 1996 with 96 pianos set on three levels. The concert started at 19:96 – that is, at 96 minutes past 7:00. The conductor was accessible via video screens and earphones. Teddy played on the first floor, and his wife (his former wife as of a few months ago), also a pianist, played on the third floor. The only audience member was a 96-year-old man, the teacher of almost all the pianists and of the composer, too. Everyone else stood outside in the rain and watched the concert on large screens.

Teddy also told us about giving a concert tour in Greenland in the late '60s. In some remote places, he said, he wasn't given a precise time or even a date for his concert. The uncertainty of the weather meant that no date could be set for anything. Instead, as soon as Teddy arrived, word flew instantly and widely: "There's a piano concert at 8:00 tonight." So well did the system work – and so rare was such a performance and so little else was there to attend – that performance halls were always full. Teddy loved playing in Greenland.

Finally it was time to leave. As we were pulling out of the driveway, Teddy came running to the car to give me a red rose he had just then picked from the garden.

The rest of the day I kicked myself for not having asked him to give us a little recital. What an opportunity thrown away to hear Denmark's leading interpreter of Chopin play a Steinway piano in his charming little house. At Kirsten's urging I called him and, after his effusive remarks about our afternoon together, said, "Teddy, I've made a terrible mistake. I didn't ask to hear you on the piano," hoping he would say, "Come over tomorrow." But he said, immediately, "Not a mistake! I haven't practiced for weeks and wouldn't have played even if you had asked." We had a nice little flirtation over the phone, then said good-bye with a promise from him to send me a CD of his renditions of the Danish Romantic composer Lange. I haven't received it yet, but I'm not worried. If he doesn't send it, I'll just pick it up the next time I'm in Skørping. This time I'll tell him in advance I'm coming, and maybe, if he practices, he'll play some Chopin for me on the Steinway piano next to the red, red roses.

A Cupboard Bed by an Ancient Hearth

For several hundred years, farmers in Sweden's Dalarna country took their cows to the mountains for summer pastures, the *fåbod*, where the women and young girls stayed to herd the cows and make cheese and butter throughout the summer. This tradition died out around 50 years ago, but even in the 19th century, *fåbod* villages such as Fryksås had become popular tourist destinations because of their beautiful old log houses and barns and their exceedingly beautiful scenery – the vast Swedish forests behind them, the heights overlooking the lakes and distant blue mountains of Dalarna, the pretty, sloping pastures with their wildflowers and slanted pole fences.

When my friend Maren and I visited Fryksås, we lodged in one of the old log houses set on a hillside. Above it four calves grazed "as of old." The small entrance hall led to a large room with a wide plank floor and, on the view side, a set of windows. Opposite the windows, a double doorway with sills worn into crescents by centuries of women's feet led to a modernized kitchen on the right and a small bedroom with a bunk bed and a small toilet room on the left. In one corner of the large room was an 18th-century cupboard bed with curtains to draw at night and, built into it at one end, a clock and a cupboard, all painted, as they originally were, in Swedish floral folk style. A long, thin wooden box on the floor next to the curtained side of the bed contained an extra eiderdown and served as a step, too, so that, as I retired that night, I was "climbing into bed" in the most literal sense of that phrase. On one side of the wide, high hearth of the stone fireplace was a 19th-century barrel-like chair, and on the other side a cupboard, painted like the bed and dated 1745. A long iron hook swung over the fireplace. The only thing missing was the cast iron pot in which the *fåbod* girls heated their water. Maren and I had the advantage of a shower and furnace later installed in the basement. From the pasture outside, cow-bells clanked and clanged, a sound familiar to this house for two or three hundred years.

Maren and I had a fabulous dinner that night at the Fryksås Hotel, overlooking the steep slope of green pastures with their old *fåbod* buildings above the more distant view of the lakes, Orsasjön and Siljan, and the blueish ring of Dalarna's mountains. At one point, the hide-and-seek of mist and sun over the fairy-tale view produced the magic of a rainbow arched over this ancient village that was as much history as it was folklore. The next night was chilly enough that Maren and I built a fire in our fireplace. It was lovely, in that centuries-old room with its beautiful old furniture, to sit at a table with candlelight, a glass of wine, good cheese and bread, watching a nearly full moon shine like spilled paint on the lake, feeling the fire warm on the hearth behind us and imagining the girls churning their butter in that room, gossiping and laughing – until the earsplitting shriek of the smoke alarm shattered the romantic atmosphere. Set off by smoke from the fireplace, the alarm drove us outdoors with our hands over our ears. The frightened proprietor came running from her *fåbod* house next door, then quickly produced a ladder and turned off the alarm. She showed us how we should have shoved the fire to the back corner of the fireplace. With the fire now burning in the proper place, she left, and Maren and I went back to our dinner and the view below. Once again we could hear the cow bells clanking outside the house. The ghosts of the *fåbod*'s girls returned to their places by the hearth, and Maren and I slipped again into 200 years of summer pasturing.

A Tale of Two Boots

It is said that if you want to know a man, walk a mile in his shoes. Does it also mean that three women linked in friendship by the same pair of boots know each other with particular insight for having walked in those boots?

Several years ago, when I was packing to go home after a sojourn in Sweden, my friend Maren, in whose house I was staying, came home in a new pair of black suede boots – short, stylish, pull-on boots with a square heel and square toes. I liked them a lot.

"Try them on," Maren said. "We wear about the same size."

She pulled the boots off her feet, and I pulled them onto mine. I turned my feet this way and that in front of Maren's mirror. The boots fit so nicely and looked so chic that I regretted not having a chance to buy a pair for myself. Maren said, "Why don't you buy mine? I'll buy another pair tomorrow."

They were such nice boots and the idea of buying them right off Maren's feet was so enticing that I did just that. We went downstairs to show my new boots to Maren's husband.

"They are very beautiful," Lasse said. "When you get back to Grants Pass, you'll be walking down the street one day and a good-looking, suave man will stop you and say, 'What nice boots! Would you like to have lunch?'"

Though Lasse's scenario never came to pass, I enjoyed wearing Maren's boots all winter. The next autumn, when I was again in Sweden, Maren and I went out together in our matching boots. I wore my boots the next winter, too, but they were beginning to hurt my feet. I had developed bunions, and finally I had to admit that I couldn't wear the boots any more. Although they were two years old by then, they hardly looked worn (I am not very hard on shoes), so this autumn when I returned to Sweden,

I brought the boots with me to give to Maren, knowing that hers were worn out. In the meantime, though, she had bought the same shoe in this year's style, so she didn't really need them, but she took them, thinking she might wear them another time.

A few weeks ago, I got an e-mail from Maren, who had just been to visit her friend Loes in Denmark, whom I know, too, and in whose house I have visited. Maren had noticed that Loes had small feet and realized they might fit in the boots I had given her, so she gave Loes the boots. "She was really happy and wore them all the time," Maren wrote. "In spite of very little money, Loes always manages to look like half a million and elegant, and the boots added to that. Imagine her in a little hat, black cape, long black skirt, and the boots. And," she added, "you even know the house where the shoes are now walking."

So it is that one pair of little black boots has linked three women in three countries with a special kinship, as each of us has walked many miles in the others' shoes.

My Father Collapses on the Streets of Italy

Last spring my mother, age 82, and my father, 91, went to Italy with my sister Sharon and her husband, Billy. They rented a car to drive through the Tuscany countryside and stayed at various *pensions*. Everywhere they went, my parents impressed people with their physical vitality and mental acuity.

Driving into one little village on streets that rapidly became more narrow than the car, Billy decided to let Mom, Dad, and Sharon walk to the church they wanted to visit while he parked the car outside town. He would join them shortly. They admired the church and then, having exhausted its tourist value, waited outside its walls for Billy. The day was hot. Suddenly my father staggered backwards. When Mom and Sharon looked up in alarm, he just said he had thought the wall was closer than it was. In the next minute he had passed out.

"Oh, my God," thought Sharon. "It's my worst nightmare – my father dying on the streets of Italy." Immediately a group of Italian workers gathered around him, waving their arms and saying the Italian equivalent of "Give him air." Someone called an ambulance, but before it arrived, my father revived. Being my father, he said, "I'm all right. Let me up," but the kind Italians insisted he stay recumbent, and when the ambulance pulled up and he said, "I don't need an ambulance," they joined my sister and mother in persuading him he should find out why he had fainted. The ambulance driver told Sharon that only one person could ride with the patient (who was my father, though he disclaimed the label). She could hardly leave Mom alone on the streets of Italy, but Mom was hardly capable of handling the situation at an Italian hospital. And where was Billy? He should have been there long ago.

At that moment, the priest stepped out of the church and offered in perfect English his assistance. "I would be glad to wait with Mrs. Coogle," he told Sharon. "You go to the hospital with your father," whereupon he turned to Mom and started chatting about Italy and the United States, taking her under his winged cassock and easing her worry with Italian charm and her own language.

At the hospital, while my father was being examined, the nurse asked Sharon the usual questions. At "How old is he?" Sharon answered in her best guidebook Italian, "Ninety-one." The nurse patiently repeated the question. Sharon, who thought she had learned Italian numbers pretty well, went over them in her head and repeated, "Ninety-one."

"No, no. You're not understanding me," the nurse said. "HOW OLD IS HE?"

Finally Sharon convinced her that the patient really was 91 years old.

Before my father returned from the examination, Billy arrived with my mother and the priest. (Billy had had his own difficulties, but that is another story.) Then my father came out of the examination room, and at this point it is necessary to interject a bit of marital history. My mother had been nagging my father for years that he should drink more water, and he, being my father, had stubbornly resisted her nagging. Now the first thing he said was, "Don't say, 'I told you so.'" He had passed out from dehydration.

The rest of the trip was flawlessly wonderful. Everyone had a good time, and my father might even have watched his intake of fluids, for he never again passed out on the streets of Italy. And my mother may – or may not – have stopped her nagging.

A Tale of Two Rings

My mother had kept her mother-in-law's wedding ring since my grandmother died in the 1940s. She and my father had also inherited his sister's husband's wedding ring. When my son, Ela, and his girl friend, Leah, decided to marry, my parents offered them those rings.

Leah picked up the rings when she was in Atlanta in March and took them to Seattle, where they went to a jeweler for resizing. From there they went to Roslyn, Washington, to David Giullietti, Ela's best friend from college and a metal engraver, who would engrave the rings with a double helix design.

David's wife, Kiva, in whose yoga class Ela and Leah had met, wrapped the engraved rings in tissue paper and carried them to the wedding in a pretty little tea box. On the day of the wedding, she gave them to another friend to display on the welcoming table at the entrance to the meadow where the ceremony would be held. But at the first curious child who grabbed the box and said, "What's this?" Louann, who felt the rings should be private until they were on the hands of the wedded couple anyway, gave them to my parents, who would be the ring bearers.

For weeks my mother had been asking, "What do ring bearers wear?" meaning, of course, octo- and nonagenarian ring bearers. She resolved the problem well, though, for the day of the wedding she and my father looked stunning in white coats and black pants with brightly colored shirts under their coats. As they walked up the spiral ramp to stand on the wedding platform with Ela and Leah, my father glowed with dignified joy, my mother with utter delight. Their white hair shone next to Ela's long red-brown hair and Leah's beautiful black hair, falling to her waist like folds of velvet.

When the minister asked for the rings, my mother, smiling mischievously, started searching her pockets. But, of course, she had the ring and gave it to Ela to slip onto Leah's finger. My father gave the other ring to Leah, who underscored her marriage vows by looking into Ela's eyes while she put the ring on his finger. Then the four of them put their left hands together in a square-dance star pattern while the minister said the appropriate words. Before my parents could leave the platform, Ela, holding Leah's hand, turned to us, the gathered circle of friends, and said, "You are looking at 59 years of marriage – and a few seconds of marriage."

In that brief moment I saw a reutterance of the vows that Ela and Leah had just made. There on the wedding platform stood the beauty of youth and the beauty of age, the glowing promise of the future in the couple being wed and the fulfillment of that promise in the two whose lives were entering a sparkling twilight. Sixty years ago next November Ela's grandparents had stood similarly before friends and family to make similar vows. They, too, had beamed with love, youth, and the promise of their lives together. Now we could see the journey Ela and Leah had vowed to take, a journey symbolized in the two rings they now wore: from that day on Vashon Island to the day 59 years hence when they would stand as my mother and father now stood, husband and wife still.

A Hero in a Windstorm

For my 60th birthday, in the third week of July, I made a backpacking trip into the Mt. Jefferson Wilderness Area with my son, Ela, and my daughter-in-law, Leah. Because the only campsites we passed were either occupied or covered with snow and because dark was hovering by the time we reached the pass, we were glad enough to find there an established campsite with several tent sites and a fire ring of large rocks, though I've never thought it a good idea to camp on a pass. We were at 7000 feet, looking directly onto the volcanic mass of Mt. Jefferson. We made camp quickly, cooked our dinners, and went to sleep under a brilliant splatter of stars. I left my tent door unzipped to witness the glaciered glory of Mt. Jefferson in the morning. But deep in the night I awoke to the first battering of a storm, rain pelting the tent with a dreadful din and drenching the bottom of my sleeping bag. I zipped the door and listened uneasily to my tent whipping in the wind.

Then the second battering began. Wind pummeled the tent, flailed at it, kicked it, beat it, shook it in its teeth like a mad dog. The wind howled, thunder rumbled, the tent flapped and thrashed with a clamor so deafening it was like being in the heart of thunder itself. Suddenly, with super strength, the wind flung one side of the tent off the ground, sending the rock anchoring that corner tumbling against my leg like a loaf of bread and the tent wall gnashing against my face. The tent undulated like an accordion. Grabbing the tent floor with both hands, I bore earthward with all my strength. I was afraid the wind would tear the tent to shreds, leaving me holding tatters of nylon ribbons streaming in the storm. I was afraid the tent would collapse, suffocating me in a billowing mound of wet nylon. Ela and Leah, awake in their tent, were imagining a third possibility, that the wind would lift the tent with me in it, tumble me head over heels, and smash me against a tree.

As though plucked from a novel, an unwelcome phrase drifted through my mind: "And the storm raged for three days." Preparing for evacuation, I held down the tent with one hand and dressed myself with the other, tying my shoes with the help of my teeth. (Thank God for yoga.) Thinking of important things in case of desperate circumstances, I put the car keys in the pocket of my rain jacket and secured my journal against my breast under the coat. Then, holding onto the tent with both hands again, I called for rescue.

"Ela!" I shouted into the storm. "I need help."

With hardly pause enough to have left his sleeping bag, Ela was at the door of my tent. "What can I do?" he yelled.

"Rocks!" I bellowed. Before the tent bucked twice again, Ela had returned with a rock too heavy for two men to carry and was thrusting it with superhuman strength into the tent wall, pushing back the wind. When I asked the next morning how he had carried such a rock, he said, "It was pure adrenaline."

He brought a second rock and then a third before I could let go of the tent and sit back. The wind hadn't diminished, but the anchors seemed to be holding. Ela returned to bed. I read an article in the *New Yorker*, then lay down to sleep.

Then the third battering began: lightning. I cowered, feeling enormously exposed, perched under low trees at the top of a pass. With three metal poles crossing over my head, I felt like a lightning rod. I unzipped the tent door and crawled into the storm. Like King Lear on the heath, I was assailed by the tempest. I watched the lightning until I was convinced it was staying about three miles away and wasn't the Zeus-throwing, cartoon-forked kind but the more benign glow variety. When I crawled into my tent to sleep at last, daylight was seeping in.

Such was the beginning of my 61st year. If it was a test, I passed with good humor. If it was indicative of storms ahead, I know I can weather them. If it was a measure of my son's love, I know I can trust it. I think it's going to be a pretty good year.

Entwined with Serpents

That the reputation of the serpent never gets redeemed after his unfortunate participation in the Eden fiasco is a pity for those of us who like snakes. I have always thought I had a psychic kinship with them, a notion that was put to the test at the Oregon Country Fair last summer when I was handed a boa constrictor.

She belonged to Reverend Chumleigh and was slung casually around his neck like a tawny laniard, sleek, clean, as thick as a man's forearm, and pure muscle. To hold her would be a hint of Eden before the Fall, but it was Chumleigh who offered, not I who asked. He unwound her from his neck and laid her in my hands, a thick, heavy, writhing vine coiling around my left arm like loops of rope, her scales smooth and tissue-paper delicate on my bare arm, her head zigzagging, her forked tongue winking in and out, her inscrutable eyes steady. Tightening against my skin in supple undulations, she slid to my shoulder. I held my arms stiffly, afraid she would startle into escape if I moved, my muscles aching from her weight. Then I thought that being a rock was wrong, that I should wave my body in matching undulations like a snake charmer's assistant or like an exotic dancer. Once at my neck the serpent settled comfortably around my shoulders like a feather boa, except there was nothing feathery about her. She was powerful with strength and purpose, never quite still without ever going anywhere. It was like bearing low-rumbling thunder on my shoulder: harmless but insinuating danger.

Years earlier I had come close another time to feeling the slick, dry contortions of a snake's body on mine. I was lying in a grassy spot near an oak tree on a mountain slope, sunning and reading. After a while I set aside my book and was half drowsing in the warm sun when some movement from a narrow fellow in the grass caught my eye. Something was gliding steadily towards me, maybe a grasshopper, I thought vaguely, ignoring, in my torporific state, the clue that grasshoppers don't glide. Idly, I let my eye follow the line of movement through the tall grass to its end closer to me, at which point torpor vanished. At the same instant that I recognized the head end of a snake two inches from my bare stomach and knew that what I had seen was the rattle end of that same snake, I was on my feet three feet away staring into the eye of a thunderously buzzing, instantly coiled rattlesnake who had simultaneously leapt three feet in the opposite direction. He had been no more aware of me as a danger than if I had been a rock.

I have wondered for years what would have happened if I hadn't startled so badly. Would I have been able to let the rattlesnake slither over my stomach as though over a rock, the way I let the boa constrictor slide up my arm? Would he have continued to think I was but a rock in his path, or would he have crawled onto my chest and suddenly frozen with fear and – and then what would he have done? What would I have done?

It's a good thing my body responds more quickly with post-Eden instincts than my affinity for snakes would allow because a rattlesnake, whatever way you look at it, is not like a pet boa constrictor.

Children in the Garden

Pushing open the wings of beautifully sculpted steel butterfly gates, my two nieces and I entered the Children's Garden of the Atlanta Botanical Gardens. And that was the end of the fun. Beyond the gates were some giant gaudy plastic figures and a short, safe children's slide. Two plastic demonstration boxes, one a boy with a circulation system, the other a flower with veins, educated us with mechanical voices. We passed by.

In Peter Rabbit's garden we stuck our heads through three holes in a wall to become the heads of the rabbit figures painted on the other side. Ha. Ha. We went into a mock Creek Indian hut, where a sign said, "Can you find five uses of plants here?" Dutifully, we did. At Grandma's Garden, we walked into a barnyard with one statue of a sheep and another of a cow, a bed of real parsley and chard, and a "Do not eat" sign. I didn't enter the open-sided hut marked "Kids only," but I could see everything, anyway, and it looked boring. Lauren and Christine didn't go in either. Another sign gave us some useless information with a word spelled wrong and an "n" turned backwards.

It was a relief to rejoin my mother and sister in the real botanical garden. As we entered, a sweet smell enticed us to look around for the December blossoms. A wide tree trunk snaking over a low wall beckoned Lauren to climb. In the tropical building, Christine and I became so enthralled by the beautiful poisonous frogs that we were still staring into their aquariums long after the rest of the family had left. Later Christine and my sister hunched in front of the orchid garden with notepads and drawing pencils while Lauren, Mom, and I meandered through a steamy jungle of tropical plants, among which dangled long ropy vines that originated, Lauren pointed out, in a particular tangle of leaves high over our heads. As we walked out of the tropical building, Christine spotted a large sculpture of the world, like a globe with crisscrossed wires on the oceans. When we discovered that it turned, I spun it like a merry-go-round with Lauren and Christine hanging onto the wires and leaping off just before they crashed into the pole.

The irony of the Atlanta Botanical Gardens is that the real garden succeeds in doing what the children's garden, with its condescending attitude and boring educational purpose, fails so miserably to do. Children's gardens, like all things made for children, should engage the imagination. The 4-H Children's Garden in Michigan is a good example. There, teddy-bear topiaries greet children at the entrance. The pizza garden is planted in slices with tomatoes, peppers, basil, and cheese-like marigolds. Children can dig up plant fossils in the Dinosaur Garden, walk into a sundial and tell time from their own shadows, touch mimosa leaves to make them curl, and follow an Alice-in-Wonderland maze. The Atlanta Botanical Garden had given my nieces (and my mother, sister, and me) the same sort of creative, interactive experience. There, Christine had done an amazing drawing of an orchid. We had discovered the source of a sweet smell in the air and had played "find the frog" in the thick vegetation of the aquarium. The children had tested their strength and daring on a spinning globe. We had played, learned things, recognized patterns of beauty, and exercised our imaginations on the environment. The Atlanta Children's Garden was an adult concept of a child's imaginative world, whereas the Botanical Garden fulfilled my ideal of a children's garden: a real world that excited and kindled a child's imagination.

Out of the Primal Ooze

As soon as Louann and I reached Big Elk Lake in the Marble Mountains Wilderness Area, I dropped my pack and hurried toward the water. Ten feet away, I became aware of a strange bubbling in the ground. When I looked closely, I saw that the bubbling was made by dozens of tiny gray-speckled frogs leaping in panic from my feet. I froze my step. Then I blinked. My focus cleared, and behold, the entire shore was thick with tiny frogs.

The foot-wide black band I had thought was muck at the edge of the water reemerged as a solid band of tadpoles, their black noses pushing toward shore, their darkly transparent tails waving good-bye to the watery womb. At the line where water met land, tadpoles turned into frogs before my eyes, like evolution in a time warp. On shore fully formed frogs swarmed like maggots. I could hear now a light buzzing in the air, the sound of great hordes of frogs leaping through grass. What I had thought was a clump of dirt in front of my arrested foot suddenly burst into motion, like popcorn in a pan, when a frog jumped onto it and set its throng of frogs to leaping, climbing on each other's backs, pushing neighbors out of the way, scrambling for footing, frantically seeking a place on an overpopulated clump of dirt, frogs falling off and shoving others off and hopping back on, slipping into and around each other until at last they found an equilibrium and were still – until the next frog on the ground below thought escape from the mob lay on the clump of dirt and jumped on, resparking the seething. A pit made by a horse print in the mud was filled with a boiling mass of frogs, trapped as if in an Edgar Allen Poe short story, desperate for escape. I wondered how deep the pit was and how many dead frogs were serving as ladders underneath leaping live frogs.

There were hundreds of thousands of frogs, each about an inch long. Because they looked like bark and because some seemed to be leaping away from the grassy shore towards the upper meadow, I guessed they were tree frogs migrating from their birthplace in the lake to life in the trees beyond the meadow. But apparently that was wrong. David Rains Wallace, in *The Klamath Knot*, relates a similar experience at the same place but calls my frogs toads. He describes the scene as "a huge, glistening mass of tiny, potbellied toads shuffling nose-to-tail out of the lake like rush-hour traffic."

Earlier in the same chapter Wallace compares the muck and mud of lakes like Big Elk to the "primal ooze." As I stood at the edge of Big Elk Lake that day with frogs in all stages of development seething around my arrested foot, I felt I had accidentally stepped into that primal ooze itself and disturbed it in all its procreative frenzy.

Disappearing Frogs

In early spring nothing is more delightful than taking a walk through the forest below my house and hearing the frogs sing from the puddles. They keep their arrhythmic beat with perfect aplomb, not one frog self-conscious about being off beat or out of tune. I stop at a distance from the puddles and listen to the loud chorus, but when I start walking again and approach closer, it is as though I am conducting Haydn's "Farewell" symphony, signaling first one member of the orchestra and then another to stop playing. Frog by frog, puddle by puddle, the music dries up.

Finally there is only one puddle before me. Its frogs are still pouring out their cacophony, and I wonder how close I can get before they, too, clam up. Trying not to vibrate the ground, I tiptoe stealthily towards the puddle, watching it hawk-eyed. Nothing moves. No frogs spring from the puddle into the woods. No splash indicates a frog has jumped into the water to escape the impending danger. The puddle is still and quiet, reflecting in its milk-brown, unwinking surface the surrounding forest with its jagged puzzle-piece of sky. I tiptoe to the edge of the puddle and peer in. I search with my eyes around its borders, paying particular attention to muddy leaves and clumps of grass and humps of harder mud and rock where a frog might lurk. I look everywhere I could possibly expect to find a frog. I look for eyes at the water's surface that would give away a camouflaged frog body. I look for big frogs and little frogs. I do the three-dimensional-picture thing with my eyes, crossing them slightly and uncrossing them to look into the puddle or onto its surface or through the water to its bottom. I stalk quietly around the edges of the puddle. I change the angle of the light according to where I stand. I stand up and look down; I squat down and look across.

I look and look and look in all possible ways, and I never see a single frog. How could they have disappeared so completely?

Finally, frogless, I turn to go home, walking back through a maze of puddles that don't give the tiniest hint, auditory or visual, of frog occupants. I stop at the same place where I had first stopped to listen to the frog chorus. I wait and wait, as unmoving as a rock or a fence post, as breathless as a tree trunk, but the frogs don't treat me to their song again. Simply by passing, I had silenced them, it seemed for the day.

It is said that frogs are disappearing all over the world. The silence from that disappearance is different from the silence and the disappearance of my frogs, who, I know, will be singing again tomorrow. No one can say exactly why frogs are disappearing, but I am not the only one to point the finger at environmental degradations. "To wantonly destroy a living species," says Thomas Berry in *The Dream of the Earth*, "is to silence forever a divine voice." It is as though we were stalking through the world, strewing silence behind us. No frog voices will swell again after we have passed in this way. This larger diminishment leaves a permanent silent spring. The silence of the frogs at my approach and their stubborn voicelessness, even when I stand completely still, is a play for my imagination, a game, a pleasure, but were this divine voice to be silenced forever, I would hear that silence loud around us, for a world without frogs is a world with a hole in its heart.

Wild Kitten

One Christmas morning when I was a child, I discovered a box with holes under the Christmas tree. I clapped my hands in glee, knowing immediately it was the kitten I had wanted. But when I reached eagerly for the box, my father stopped me. He told me he had found this tiny kitten wild in the alleys of Atlanta near his earmold laboratory. He had caught her, but she had escaped the box and created havoc in the lab. He and an employee had had to put on gloves to catch her again. If I wanted this kitten for a pet, he said, I would have to tame her.

What an enchantment this was! All other Christmas gifts were forgotten as I took the box to my bedroom and closed the door. When I opened the box, a fuzzy, gray, wild-eyed little creature shrank against the cardboard, hissing and snarling. I went to the kitchen for milk for her, but when I came back she was gone. I lifted the valance of my bed, and she stared at me from the darkness with wild, distrustful eyes.

For days, weeks, and months I worked to gentle my kitten, whom I named Pokey (because she was so fast, I said, playing with irony). Finally the day came when she let me touch her, then the day when she accepted my caresses and a place in my lap. She ran under the bed at the sound of the vacuum cleaner or when anyone else came in the room, but she would let me crawl after her and pull her out. As the years went by, she gradually allowed other members of the family to pet her, too, and after many, many years, she grudgingly accepted strangers.

She was supposed to be an outdoor cat, but when she jumped onto the outer sill of my bedroom window at night, I would let her in to sleep with me, keeping my door closed so my mother wouldn't know. During one such night, as I stroked Pokey in my half-sleep, she purred especially loudly. In the morning I discovered to my utter surprise four kittens lying with her on my bed. Terrified that my mother would discover I had broken the rules, I placed Pokey and her kittens in a box and washed out my sheets. But, of course, my mother saw the sheets hanging over the shower rod, and I had to confess that Pokey had birthed kittens in my bed.

I had to leave my cat behind when I went to college. One day I got a letter from my mother telling me that Pokey had died. "She wandered into the woods," my mother said, "and never came back."

A wild kitten in the beginning, Pokey had died in the way of wild creatures. I felt a twinge of sadness. This was the cat I had tamed, the cat who had taught me that love and care and tenderness can win a creature's trust and that patience is a virtue. This cat had distinguished me from all other humans with her love. She had trusted me when she trusted no one else. That was when I was a child. I was grown up now and going the way of adulthood, but Pokey's death gave me pause to consider the girl who preceded the woman. I knew then – and I know now – that no Christmas gift of my childhood was ever more meaningful than that box with holes in it and its little wild kitten.

Photographed at 82

My niece Cameron, a photography student, distributed her Christmas gifts with eagerness: portrait photographs of her grandparents. These close-up head shots of my mother and father are marvelous! Both faces are alive with curiosity and interest; the eyes sparkle with vitality. It is remarkable to think these people are 82 and 90 years old. They look decades younger.

But my mother took one look at her picture and fled in horror. Did she really look like that? She peeked in her bedroom mirror. Oh, yes! It was true! A wrinkled old woman – that is what people saw when they looked at her – and Mom wept alone in her bedroom Christmas morning.

That's where Cameron found her, and when she understood why her grandmother was crying, she started to cry, too, at this unexpected reaction to the gift she had thought so precious.

"But, Grandma, I think you're beautiful!" she told her.

My mother gestured toward the picture. "Beautiful? Hardly!"

It was a Christmas crisis, but Mom and Cameron wiped their tears and rejoined the gaiety in the next room to enjoy the day. Nonetheless, Mom really was deeply upset. Later, when she could talk about it more evenly, she told me, unconsciously echoing Dickens, "It was the best and the worst Christmas present I've ever received – to face reality."

But she had seen other pictures of herself. Why did this one cause such a shock? "The others were snapshots," she said, "flashbulb pictures." They weren't as revealing as this one. But did she never look in the mirror? Did she not know what she looked like? "No one likes to have her blemishes so exposed," she told me.

Blemishes? I studied the picture again. It was true that the skin wasn't smooth over the upper lip and a few lines stretched into the forehead, but I've seen more lines on the face of a 50-year-old. I would do well to look this good at 82. Why couldn't Mom see how beautiful she looked in this portrait? Maybe it was the difference between feeling on the inside and seeing from the outside. Obviously the woman in the photograph had not succumbed to the idea of old age, so maybe my mother, who has the vitality of a 30-year-old, feels closer to 30 than to 80, so maybe to see herself looking older than 30 was a shocking glimpse of reality. But what did she expect an 80-year-old woman to look like? When we are 80, do we still think beauty is only defined by the qualities of sexual attraction that delineate the procreation of the race? Without the clear skin, abundant hair, plump lips, and all the rest that nature endowed woman with in order to attract the male beast to her lair, is there nothing of beauty left to us?

This photograph is the very proof that there is. Mom's eyes glow with good humor, interest, fascination. Her mouth, closed, stretches into a smile that illuminates her entire face, lighting up every line with delight. She is not exhibiting an expression of an old woman. If youthfulness is defined by a delight with life and a mind engaged with excitement, then this photograph depicts a woman still young, no matter how many wrinkles we might count. This is a beautiful woman. Anyone would say so.

Meeting the Earth Goddess

Several years ago I went to Los Angeles to visit a man I had met several times but didn't know well and who hadn't yet fallen into the category of "not a friend." To my disappointment and restless displeasure that weekend, he turned out to be both a bore and a boor, so when he took me to Santa Monica Beach and fell snoringly asleep on my beach towel, I was more relieved than annoyed.

The sand was sparkling white, the ocean a rippling blue. The surf swelled green, then rolled over to pound foamy white, recede, and start again with an undular rhythm that said *on and on and on the same*. A woman walked past and into the ocean. With her entrance into this elemental scene, all other figures faded and disappeared. She, alone, walking with slow, graceful steps, belonged in this scene. With every step she made, the sand trembled. The ocean rolled to every rhythmic roll of her hips. She wore a bikini. She had shoulder-length black hair, rather ordinary shoulders and waist, and enormous hips, round, smooth, rolling hips. She had thighs that embraced the ocean.

Hers was the beauty of the fecundity of this earth, its richness and feminine birthingness, its oceans and skies and mountains. Hers was the beauty of all the procreative joy of the universe. Without her, we wither. Hers was a beauty of form our ancient forebears knew and worshiped. She was the walking embodiment of the ancient earth goddess.

Hers was not the beauty of the "perfect" figure, and I wondered how a man would see her. Would he dismiss her with disdain as "too fat"? Did she in her childhood decry her big-bottomed figure, wish for the Miss America body, deny her own beauty? Did she at some time in her life try to hide this beauty in cover-up clothes? Oh, damn the culture that would shame such beauty!

But now she carried herself like the earth goddess she was; she walked with a step that riveted eyes to her. How had she overcome, even superseded, the reign of the Hollywood image? Had she recognized herself in those drawings of fertility goddesses? Had she been to Esalen and learned that the body that is loved and cared for is beautiful? Or was she of a cultural heritage (Hawaiian, perhaps) in which a different body type – hers – was the epitome of beauty rather than the Venus shape modern Western culture demands?

Brian awoke and apologized for having gone to sleep. "What a bore I am," he said with more truthfulness than he knew.

The earth goddess rose from the ocean and walked up the beach past us. Brian didn't notice her, and I didn't point her out to him. "Look," I wanted to say – but didn't want to say. "Isn't she beautiful?" I wanted to worship her, to thank her for giving us this shape, this beauty, and I was afraid the man beside me would say, "God! Look at those hips, wouldja!"

But this man was a boor as well as a bore. What did he know about beauty? As we left the beach, I saw my earth goddess reclined on her towel, two young men hovering over her. Perhaps, then, there are those who still worship the beauty of the earth goddess, and our sense of the varying beauty of the feminine form may have some hope of surviving the dominant image favored by the Western male ego.

Goldilocks in Golden's House

Because Ashland is an hour's drive from my deep-in-the-mountains home, if I know I'm going to be in town until late at night, I'll often ask an Ashland friend for a place to stay overnight. Before one particular concert in Ashland I contacted friends there who had offered such a place. John said certainly I could stay there that night, and because I had never been to his house before, he gave me detailed directions. "The guest room has a separate entrance," he explained, "so you can park by the porch. Walk down the pea gravel, then down the steps to the guest room. We'll be asleep, but I'll leave the porch light on. I'll set out a pillow for you." He told me how to identify his driveway. "It might be hard to find in the dark," he warned. He said Jeff Golden, a Jefferson Public Radio political show host and one-time county commissioner, lived next door.

It was after eleven when I started down John's street. After the bend, I looked for the truck, then counted two driveways past it and saw the telephone pole with the steel box and three reflectors. To the left of the pole was the driveway. I did not see the Joe Charter campaign sign, but I figured I had missed it in the dark, so I went down the driveway.

I parked by the front porch, where the light was on. I had thought John meant a light at the guest room, but maybe I had misunderstood. I sat in the car, hoping this was the right house, but when nothing happened, I started down the gravel and arrived at a little guest house. There were no steps, but there was a little incline. Was that what John had meant? I took a deep breath at the threshold. If the door was locked, I would know I was wrong. I turned the knob. The door opened. I walked in and switched on the light.

Hm. John hadn't mentioned that the house was still under construction, but he had only recently built his house, so

I wasn't too surprised. There was a couch in the front room. I had expected a bed, but John had told me to bring my sleeping bag, so maybe I had made an assumption. I was sorry to see he had forgotten the pillow.

Tiptoeing through the half-finished little house (hoping the three bears wouldn't come home), I found a bathroom, unfinished but apparently usable. Then I sat tentatively on the couch and waited. Nothing happened, so I shook out my sleeping bag, took out my contact lenses, and was just starting to undress when there was a knock on the door.

It was John. "You're in the wrong house!" he said. "This is Jeff Golden's house."

Oh, my God, I really was Goldilocks!

I jumped up in alarm and gathered my things. John was agitatedly pointing out everything that didn't match his directions. Reacting defensively, I jabbered excuses – it was hard to see my way in the dark, it was easy to misunderstand telephone directions, my memory is poor. Then I realized that he was saying, "It's not my fault," and that my saying, "I'm not as dumb as it seems," implied that it was his fault, so I just let it be and thanked him for rescuing me. He told me that Jeff was gone for the weekend, so I might as well leave my car where it was. I followed him a short distance, stepping over the little fence into his yard, where everything fell visually into place: the parking space next to the porch, the light on at the guest room, the pea gravel leading to the steps. The room was fully constructed and had a real bed, with a pillow. There were towels in the bathroom.

I slept soundly that night in the proper bed. I did have a strange dream, though, with images of Jeff Golden coming home to find a bear in his bed.

The Backhoe and the *Sagrada Familia*

One day, as I was stopped by a flagger holding up traffic for road construction, I watched a backhoe at work, roaring and screeching as it maneuvered expertly about the job. How many workers, I wondered, had that machine displaced? Were they glad not to be digging ditches any more? Or did they resent the machine because when jobs had called for a pick and a shovel, they could get an honest day's work for an honest day's wage? Were they angry to have been shunted aside, their expertise suddenly superfluous, their knowledge dangling uselessly from idle hands? The man with a mattock is gone from this landscape. Now it's the backhoe, the cat, and the bulldozer that work on our roads.

Once I stood in the construction rubble of the *Sagrada Familia*, a church in Barcelona, Spain, designed in 1883 by Gaudi and still unfinished. Only the east façade, the Portal of the Nativity, stood completely finished, a fairy-tale marvel of intricate lacy concrete and stone, highly decorated with sculptures, statues, and the frilly scrollwork the Swedish call *snickerglädje*, "carpenter's fun," when it's found on wooden buildings. The tall, pointed steeples rose up like ornate pinnacles around the ghostly future of the rest of the church, whose vague outlines nevertheless suggested the Gothic size of the prospective building. While I stood there in the ruins of this vast structure that hadn't been built yet, in a church that was still more imagination and faith than stone and concrete, I heard the slow tap! tap! tap! of one solitary stonemason at work. In that sound I sensed, behind me, the decades of the building in progress and, before me, more decades of this building in progress, another hundred years of the slow emergence into being of Gaudi's lofty ideas. In the emptiness between the strikes of the hammer I saw the Medieval cathedrals – Chartres, Rouen, Cologne – a hundred years or more in the building. It was a solitary, tiny sound that returned to me now in "that inward eye/which is the bliss of solitude" as I sat in my car on a country road in Oregon, listening to the sound of another solitary worker: the loud roar of the late 20th century.

Delighted, Then Decimated, by Daffodils

One winter years ago, my funds were at such a low ebb that I closed my little house on the mountain and took a Greyhound bus to Atlanta, where I worked two jobs: in the evenings as a waitress in a pizza restaurant near Emory University and during the day as a secretary at my father's ear-mold laboratory. Living with my sister helped me bear the tedium of being in the city, and I found waitressing both interesting and lucrative. Although I don't care for secretarial tasks, working for my father had personal as well as monetary rewards. But I missed my son and my home and longed for the time I could return.

One of the things that helped me endure those months in Atlanta was to walk to work each morning. I enjoyed the exercise, the outdoors, and the one-mile walk through a black neighborhood of old houses with little, well-kept yards. My route crossed a large vacant lot before melding into the crowded streets of downtown Atlanta. Two things on this walk brought me particular joy: a stone wall draped with lavender thrift and other rock garden flowers, and, on the vacant lot, a host of golden daffodils. The old mansion on the site had long since been razed. Now the only remnant of its domestication was this garden of daffodils. Cheerful and bright amid the rubble and debris of a cleared lot, they bespoke spring, flowers, and gardens. They brought an extra lilt to the heart of any passerby. For me in particular they were a reminder of the tenacity of beauty while I was in the foreign landscape of the city. They whispered to me I would be home again soon. Every few days I picked three or four daffodils for a vase on my office desk, where they brightened my day, eased my work, and seemed to shorten the distance between me and my home, my son, and my own garden.

One day on my way to work, I walked into the vacant lot as usual, but the daffodils were gone. Someone had picked every last flower. It's true these daffodils belonged to me no more than to that picker, but I felt desecrated. Now I had no daffodils to remind me of gardens while I worked at a desk. I could no longer smell their sweet fragrance while the electric tools of the lab growled and whined behind me. The joy had been bleached from my walk. I would have been glad to share the daffodils, day after day, bud into bloom, with anyone who wanted a few for the home or office. There were plenty for all – until this one person gathered all the pleasure unto herself, leaving the passersby whose steps had been lightened by daffodils suddenly bereft.

Working with my Father

My father is a man rich with humor, but also silent, a man who throughout his life didn't understand small talk and seemed to me in many ways socially inept. He rarely talked about himself, and for years I only knew Ken Coogle the father, the man who roughhoused with his children on the living-room floor, who took us camping and canoeing, who chaired the after-Sunday-dinner family council meetings in a manner both patriarchic and democratic, listening to the objections and complaints of his children, their accomplishments and desires, their carefully researched and outlined requests for bigger allowances. But the private man? Ken Coogle outside the family? Who was he?

To say that he was owner and manager of Eveready Plastics, a small lab that made earmolds for hearing aids, would seem only to categorize him, yet it was in that setting, when I worked for him as a teen-ager, that I began to know him differently. Letters in the files attested to his honesty and fairness, his high morals in the competitive world of business. By their presence and respect, employees attested to his active sense of social justice. One employee he helped through struggles with alcoholism. Another was a black man. Even though at that time in Georgia if a black man worked in a business he was the janitor, in my father's office Henry was a lab technician on equal footing with the others. Henry named his first son after my father. Just after the birth, my father and I went to see this little black baby named Ken. I was uncomfortable being in the black ghetto of Atlanta for the first time and in the private home of Henry and Naomi, but that discomfort was nothing next to my shock at seeing that the baby cradled in Naomi's arms wasn't black. I blushed and stammered and hung back, at a loss for social graces. My father, on the other hand, whom I had thought so socially inept, was gracious and at ease, saying, "What a fine baby!" playfully letting little Ken's fist wrap around his finger. He seemed pleased. Henry and Naomi were beaming proudly. As Dad and I left the house, he explained that dark pigment increases as the baby ages and assured me his namesake really was a black boy.

I am my father's daughter, though, and during all those years I worked for him, I never opened myself to him any more than he to me. Once when we were driving home from work, with the car stopped in rush-hour traffic and me far away in my teen-age thoughts, he tossed a penny into my lap. "That's for your thoughts," he said.

In my unforgivably impertinent teen-age way, I returned the penny, replying tartly, "My thoughts are worth more than a penny." What I threw away with that returned penny was worth a great deal more than my petty thoughts.

I worked with as well as for my father in the lab and in the office, but the best times were in the basements – the basement of the office where his printing press sat and the basement of the house where he kept his woodworking tools and winemaking equipment. By being with him in those basements, I learned something about woodworking, printing, and winemaking, but it was the ineffable lessons of those hours that meant the most to me, the unspoken lessons in how to become a worthwhile adult.

He never went to church. Every Sunday morning as the rest of us trooped out the front door in our Sunday finery bound for Peachtree Road Methodist Church, he disappeared to the basement in his old white T-shirt. One warm spring Sunday, years after I had grown up and was now home for a visit, I went in search of my father after my mother had left for church. I found him repairing the flagstone walk to the front door and offered my assistance. I worked there with him without many words, as in the past, now sharing my father's sacred hours. In a rare move towards verbal intimacy, he spoke about his father. Could I redeem now the lost penny of my childhood?

"He was a brick mason," Dad told me. (I hadn't known that!) "He didn't want his children to be brick masons, too."

"Why not?" I asked.

"He wanted something better for them," my father said.

Was the owner of a small business that made earmolds better than a bricklayer? Was a teacher/writer better than a businessman? Is the value of a man to be measured by the way he earns a living? Conversations with my father tended to leave the depths opened but nonverbalized. A man of few words, he was a teacher of many values. If I am my father's daughter, I would I could emulate him there.

Generational Differences

Until I went to college, I was a model child. I got along well with my mother. At college, however, I began exerting my independence, exploring paths she considered socially or morally unacceptable. Trouble erupted. She clutched and clung, and the wilder my flight the deeper her claws. The deeper her claws, the more determined I seemed not merely to untie the umbilical cord but to hack it to bits.

Each generation wrenches away from the one before, but I think my generation was exceptionally pugnacious and rebellious. As a child of the '60s, given my taste for adventure and my intellectual bent, it was perhaps inevitable that I would join the back-to-the-land movement. Just as inevitably, because she was a parent in the '60s and had strong mothering instincts and a directive nature, my mother became overwhelmingly bewildered as she tried desperately to hold me in the fold, the fence of which I had already jumped.

The sexual revolution was much to blame. Nothing had prepared my mother for such brash behavior. When I came home from a semester in France, she told me, with disgust, "You learned to dress sexy in France."

What's wrong with that? I wondered, feeling I had cast off the last threads of dowdiness.

Two years later I graduated from Vanderbilt University with a two-year scholarship at Cambridge University. Before I left for England, one of my professors, who had befriended me well at Vanderbilt, opened my eyes a little over lunch one day in the university cafeteria. "You know what she's afraid of, don't you?" he asked. I didn't know, so he told me. "She's afraid you'll have sex before you get married."

I was naive enough at that time to scoff at that fear. He, however, knew me well enough, and knew the world well enough, and knew the changing times well enough to raise an eyebrow at my skepticism. He was right, of course. Overseas, on my own, among sophisticated contemporaries, I became a part of the sexual revolution.

Back in the States two years later, I became an eager participant in the cultural revolution as well. My mother's agony proved my mettle, verified my membership. But as the years went by, I became less belligerent in my independence, less caustic in my responses to her bellicosity. In turn, she began to accept that my choices, however wrong, were at least mine. As the years mellowed our differences, I softened towards her, finally allowing myself to remember it was she who taught me that to hold the hand of a child is good and to give to a neighbor in need is to do no more than what is asked of a neighbor. I began to be grateful for the sense of linear family she had given me and to realize it was something the hippie family could never replace. I may have felt I had learned a lot from encounter groups and Zen Buddhism about living and being, but without my mother's convictions and faiths I might have lost a good deal I have cherished. This sense of family is a valuable thing to have given my son, too. I am glad "grandmother" and "aunt," "grandfather" and "uncle" were meaningful terms while he was growing up. I am thankful that a sense of generations will keep us all in our place.

Peggy Chatham, Nobody

Peggy Chatham was not in the "in" crowd of Miss Cunningham's second-grade class. Fat, sour-smelling, and pasty-skinned, she wore shabby non-fashions and faded into the washed-out edges of class pictures. When we played hopscotch at recess, she melted into the background. When we swang on the swings, no one pushed her. When we giggled and gossiped, she saw only our backs and heard nothing but indistinct whispers. She never raised her hand in class, and she never won races or played the Littlest Angel in the Christmas pageant. Peggy Chatham was a nobody, a loser, a person who grows up thinking life belongs to someone else.

For Easter Miss Cunningham's class made bonnets from paper plates dribbled and draped with crepe paper ribbons and fancied up with paper doilies and pastel paper flowers. Afterwards, we marched around the room to the scratchy tune of "Easter Parade" on a tinny record player while Miss Cunningham judged our marvelous creations. She would give a prize to the best milliner. As we paraded, I compared hats of the possible competition – Mary Lou Johnston's maybe or Amelia McKoy's. Like me, these friends were always winners. But my hat was better than theirs. Smug in my self-assurance, I paraded my hat.

"And first-place winner," said Miss Cunningham, "is Peggy Chatham."

Peggy Chatham? That shabby, faceless vagueness? That fat wispiness who never played our games or read out loud in class? That who? The fire of my face threatened to reveal my shame – not that I hadn't won but that I had assumed I would. My vanity scathed me, scalded my body with hot, sudden sweat. Thick tears of embarrassment burned my eyes. No one was watching me; they were all watching her, so, risking detection, I shot a glance at this new Peggy Chatham. There she was, in her paper hat no better than mine, her hand outstretched to receive her Easter candy prize from a smiling Miss Cunningham, her face beaming while mine was burning.

A child in a child's world, I hadn't learned yet there might be value in the Peggy Chathams who hung around its edges. Now, adult, I know the "of course" behind the choosing of Peggy Chatham. Any teacher with an eye on the personal dynamics of the class, any adult with an understanding of the value of a prize to a forgotten child, any god with an awareness of what it means to turn a nobody into a sunbeam of significance would have done the same.

I would like to say I was instantaneously transported into the awareness of adulthood, that with Peggy Chatham's elevation out of the slough of nothingness, I was likewise delivered from the gutter of arrogance and conceit, but the transformation wasn't that dramatic. I didn't take Peggy Chatham's hand to congratulate her, to draw her into the "in" crowd, or to beg her forgiveness. It was not I, but Miss Cunningham, who made a difference to Peggy Chatham, for if the most deadly phrase of Peggy's adulthood might have been "I've been a loser all my life," Miss Cunningham stabbed it in the heart before it could take root there and consume her like a bosom serpent.

.

A Little Gray Flower and the Celtic Mermaid

My Danish friend Kirsten and I took a walk one day while I was visiting her, heading for a swim in a lake. Before we emerged from the forest, we came upon a little house by the railroad tracks where two of Kirsten's friends lived: Inger, a national champion sculler, currently a Forest Service intern, and Zinta, a stone carver.

"Hello!" Kirsten shouted from the gate.

A young woman came running from the house to greet her. "Oh, Kirsten! Hello! Hello!" she effused. When she turned to me, I introduced myself, saying, "I'm Diana."

She grabbed my hand, gazed adoringly into my eyes, and cried, "Oh, you're Diana! I've been wanting to meet you!"

I was taken aback by such unexpected familiarity and enthusiasm for my name. Thinking Kirsten must have been telling tales of my swimming exploits, I said, confusedly, "Kirsten has told you about me, then?"

"Oh, no," she said, her eyes sparkling with delight. "I read your book!"

This was Zinta. We chatted a few minutes there at the gate. Then Kirsten and I continued our walk to the lake and had a good swim. No one was home when we passed the little railroad house on the return.

The next day Zinta called and asked to speak to me. "I have a gift for you," she said. "It's a stone carving of a Celtic mermaid. It's unfinished, but if you want it and can take it home, I'll work on it this afternoon, and you can pick it up later in the day."

If I wanted it? I didn't know how I would carry home such a heavy thing as a carved stone slab, but such a gift could not be left behind. Late that afternoon Kirsten and I walked through heavy rain to the railroad house, where the over-exu-

75

berant Zinta and the quiet, strong Inger met us at the door. Divesting us of our wet clothes, they ushered us through a tiny kitchen vestibule into a little square house, very warm and jam-packed more with cardboard boxes than with furniture. Kirsten and I sat cheek to jowl on a small sofa behind a coffee table. Zinta danced nervously in front of it while Inger observed us with big, brown, steady eyes from a table in a corner, camou-flaged by stacks of boxes. At the window a black cat snoozed on a green velvet pillow.

Zinta proudly presented to me the Celtic Mermaid. Cut in relief on a piece of black slate 18 inches square, the Mermaid holds her braids, looped into symmetrical Celtic knots, in uplift-ed hands. Her double tail coils beneath her in two similar Celtic knots. The local gravedigger, digging up sites to make room for new graves, had given the stone to Zinta, asking only that she erase all evidence of its writing. The back of the Celtic Mermaid had been routed clean. She was exquisitely carved. Zinta rubbed oil over the surface of the stone to make her stand out darkly brilliant.

Zinta chattered nervously in bolts and starts. Her name, she said, was Latvian and meant "little gray flower." She had grown up fatherless in Canada and had finally, disappointingly, met her father in Latvia. The house where she and Inger lived had been the home of railroad engineers of the 19th and 20th centuries. She had taken an apprenticeship in stone carving, a career with scarce employment but an art she loved with zealotry. She had wanted to carve the Celtic Mermaid ever since she found the design years ago in a Celtic design book. Now she darted all over the room looking for the book until Inger slid it wordlessly into her hand. Zinta told me she had been inspired to carve the Celtic Mermaid at last after reading my book, but after two hours she had quit working on it. Then she met me in per-son and knew what she wanted to do with the Celtic Mermaid. Today she had worked in the rain for six more hours to finish it for me.

Inger came from behind the table and talked about rowing. Danish rowers were the best competitors in bad weather, she said, because they were so used to it. Having always trained on the sea, she was caught by surprise at the heaviness of her boat on fresh water. She had rowed in competitions all over the world. Then Zinta butted in to say that Inger had given up rowing when she met her. "I'm afraid it was my fault," she said, not guiltily, as she meant it, but proudly, adoringly. Kirsten and I mumbled something appropriate – Inger was doing what she wanted; she would row again when they lived closer to water – but Inger just looked at Zinta steadily and lovingly. When Zinta threw herself into Inger's arms ("comfort me, be my security, don't go away"), Inger gave us a swift glance that said, "I love her. I know exactly who she is. Isn't she being silly? Of course, I accept her like this." It struck me that boating was the perfect metaphor for this relationship – Inger steady, sure, and unflinching through all the Zinta storms; Inger the protector, the provider, the hand on the tiller.

When it was time for me to return to the United States, my friend Lasse wrapped the Celtic Mermaid, heavy as an anchor, in layers of cardboard. He secured the package with rope and looped the rope into a handle. For the next 30 hours I lugged my precious Mermaid and my suitcases from car to airplane, from one airplane to another, from airplane to bus to car. Finally I carried her in my arms up the hill to my house. She has found her place just outside my front door under a climbing rose. From this spot she brings to my garden not only Celtic lore and veneration for nature but also the spirit of a little gray flower, lovingly protected, in a little house next to the railroad tracks in the Danish woods.

Family Greetings at the Airport

When I was at an airport recently, waiting for a friend to arrive, I witnessed two family dramas. In the first, a young man walked off the plane and greeted an older man, obviously his father. They spoke amicably to each other – "How was your flight?" "Do you have any luggage?" "Are you tired?" – but they never touched. They not only never embraced; they never even shook hands. Oh, hug him! hug him! I silently urged, but they just stood next to each other and talked. Then the mother came up, and – same thing! Finally, she did give the son a little hug. This scene may not have indicated family hostility, but oh! how I missed its family warmth.

Then I saw a small boy, seven or eight years old, just off the plane, sobbing hard in the arms of his mother. He was clinging tightly to her, his head pressed against her bosom and his arms clutching her as if never to let go. He was telling her through his sobs something about having gotten on the wrong plane. He must have been a minor traveling alone and had been put on the wrong plane at a layover. Everything was all right now, but I felt so sorry for him; it had all been so awful. His mom was saying, over and over, "I'm so glad you're here. I'm so glad you're here." But, still crying as though heartbroken, he wailed, "And I wanted to run to you, and I didn't get to!"

"You wanted to run to me?" she asked, holding him a little away from her so she could look at him. "Stay right here," she said and turned and walked away while he stood in place, a little anxiously and a little curiously. When she was a good 50 feet away, she turned around and said, "Okay, one, two, three –." The little boy's face lit up with a radiant smile. He ran straight into his mother's arms, full of happiness at the expected reunion. And oh, how I loved that mother.

Christmas with Family

On Christmas morning 1997, I was in my parents' house in Georgia, the same house in which the Coogle children were raised, the same house where we had for so many years kept our Christmas customs. This day began, as Christmas did when I was a child, with waiting. Would my sisters never arrive? When we were five children in this same house, it was we who were impatient and Mom and Dad who had to keep us from dashing downstairs to the Christmas tree before they had turned on the Christmas lights and set out Santa Claus's presents. Now presents were jumbled in a huge pile under the Christmas tree, glowing with lights in the upstairs sunporch, where my son, my sister, her husband, and I waited calmly.

"Where are they?" Dad asked fretfully, as though we were children again and couldn't be held back after the appointed time. He who had taught me the virtue of patience seemed impatient this morning. But maybe time drags as much for the 90-year-old as for the nine-year-old.

"Looks like you did a lot on the puzzle yesterday," I said to him. The distraction succeeded; Dad joined me at the table to work on this year's jigsaw puzzle. Mom was banging pans in the kitchen. I knew by the sound that she thought someone should be there helping her. Sharon left her seat next to Billy and went into the kitchen. Ela played my guitar. Dad and I worked on the puzzle.

At last everyone arrived. "Merry Christmas! Merry Christmas!" Coats were discarded. Hugs were given. Laura grabbed Sharon and disappeared into the bedroom for Christmas secrets. Linda and Bruce put more packages under the tree. My niece Cameron hung at the edge of the melee, still a teen-ager embarrassed by family. The male cousins filled the room with their big bodies, their booming voices. Dad was standing in the hall. "Well, come on. Come on," he said, trying to move us towards the stockings ritual. Laura and Sharon rejoined the throng in the hall.

"Line up," Dad said. "Youngest first." That's the way it always was when we were children: Lee, the youngest, at the head of the line, then Laura, Sharon, Diana, Linda. Now, even though it didn't matter any more, we jostled for position again, then marched in line into the living room, where the stockings were, in fact, hung over the fireplace. Mom used to be the stockings stuffer, but now we draw names and create marvelous, well-stuffed stockings for each other.

When the room was littered with paper, ribbon, and small presents, we abandoned it to its mess and gathered around the Christmas tree. When we were children, Dad always played Santa Claus, picking up the presents from under the tree, reading the names, handing out gifts, so, in keeping with tradition, he played that role again. But he isn't as fast as he used to be, and Mom, growing impatient, snatched a present to give to someone, usurping Santa Claus's job, insulting the master of ceremonies. Ela stepped in, a more diplomatic Santa's helper, to calm ruffled egos and speed things up. Chaos reigned again for a while as we opened presents, squealed, hugged, laughed, put on hats and muumuus, tried games, blew new whistles, and piled our presents next to us, mashing wrapping paper into empty boxes (the neater ones) or leaving it on the floor (those who think neatness isn't appropriate on Christmas).

At last, all the presents were open, and the excitement died down. Then, more quietly, we praised, laughed, and thanked all over again. Dad sat in his chair trying out a new gimmick. Mom disappeared into the kitchen. Some of the daughters followed, and in no time banana bread, sausage and scrambled eggs, biscuits, fresh fruit, coffee, and orange juice adorned the sunporch table.

It was a good Christmas breakfast, much as usual. It was a good Christmas, too, again this year. It's a good Christmas tradition we have in our family. It's a good family.

Christmas Hoo-Hah

In an effort to reduce the unwieldy number of gifts he feels obligated to give at Christmas, my nephew Darryl sent a family-wide e-mail well before the next Christmas. "Change is good, right?" he began and went on to propose, first, that we do away with our years-long tradition of drawing names for stockings and, second, that we divide the family into the Cousin Coogles (his generation) and what he called (affectionately, he said) the Crusty Coogles (the older generations). Each level would draw names for a gift exchange.

Protests poured in. First of all, the Crusty Coogles objected strenuously to their designation. One sister wrote, "Am I that cranky a curmudgeon?" My brother wrote, "Crusty Coogles (humph)" and redesignated us the "Coogle Upper Crust."

The Upper Crust immediately rejected the name draw, opting to continue giving gifts to each other, as per hundreds of years. The Cousins could draw names if they liked. Apparently the stocking tradition is dear to the hearts of all. My niece Cameron wrote, "I love stockings! Christmas would be a sad day without them." Her brother Dave made an impassioned plea for stockings in spite of what he called "an egregious proportion of office supplies to the amount of time any Coogle descendant EVER spends in an office. And it is my stated opinion," he went on, "that no personal hygiene product should be wrapped up and passed off as a 'present' in public, as has been the case on many a Christmas day." He remarked on the true creativity that goes into our stockings – theme stockings, hand-made-gift stockings, collaborative efforts – but he suggested that, in case some of these "meticulous orchestrations" scared some people off, anyone attempting to be too creative would have to host the annual Coogle Talent Show, by which allusion, he admitted, he was "shamefully entering a plea for the reestablishment of this tradition which has been unjustly squelched by a few nameless sourpusses."

My sister Sharon's reply to this last was that she would begin practicing her arias, a move greeted with meaningful silence.

My sister Laura said she was confused. She had thought Santa Claus did the stockings, but, now that the cat was out of the bag ("or the elf out of the stocking," she said), she suggested we exchange stockings only among the people who would be sharing Christmas at Mom and Dad's house in Atlanta. I vehemently opposed that idea for obvious reasons.

My brother was "bothered by the idea of reducing gift-giving to a formula expressed in GUPPIES (gift units per people in extraordinary stress)." My sister Sharon said that whatever the rules were, she might just be giving gifts to anyone she wanted to, anyway. But however we resolve the gift-giving issue, one thing is clear: we are a family who love a creative exchange, whether of ideas, words, or stockings.

Circles

For their wedding, my son and his fiancee asked me to write something about circles – the theme of the wedding – to read during the ceremony. It was my great honor to ascend the spiral wedding platform, centered in a wide circle of family and friends seated in a meadow, and read these words:

A circle is a geometric figure of wholeness, the completion of a curve.

A great curve of binding energy holds the universe together in its wholeness.

We are born whole from the circle of the womb, and from that moment we live in the circle of breath.

The blood in our bodies moves in a circle, the same life-giving blood, day after day, year after year, renewed with every circle home again to the heart.

The heart is the center of the circle.

Like the blood in our bodies, the water of the rivers starts in the heart of the mountain and flows through all the limbs of the earth to the ocean, where it joins the cycles of the tides and, having first evaporated into air and then condensed into rain, returns to the heart. All the water of the earth, like all the blood of the body, is always the same, returning again and again, renewed, to bring life to the body of the earth.

The sun is a circle, and although we sometimes see the moon as a sickle, it, too, is a circle, and these two circles move through the heavens in a circular pattern.

The earth is a circle. Like a whirling Sufi, ecstatic it spins, giving us from that ecstasy the cycle of night and day.

An orbit is a circle. From the orbit of the Earth come the cycle of seasons and the circular turning of the stars in the sky.

A round is a circle, whether it is a part of a log to chop or a kind of music.

A wheel is a circle that moves. Thousands of years ago some prehistoric hunters, resting, exhausted, as they carried home their kill, saw a round stone with a hole in it and, sticking a log through the hole, discovered the wheel. From that simple moment, for better or worse, have come carriages and carts, wagons, automobiles, wheelbarrows, bicycles, skates and skateboards, trains and airplanes, baby strollers, dollies, pull toys, wheelchairs, desk chairs, vacuum cleaners – more wheeled objects than are dreamt of in your philosophy, Horatio.

But the wheel is no longer just a circle that moves to transport people or goods. Ela has reinvented the wheel as a circle that moves to make music in instruments like the Orbitone, Lunatone, Rumitones, and Rainhoops.

A ball is a circle, and a hoop is a circle. In the game of basketball, players run in circles with a ball from hoop to hoop.

Sewing circles make quilts, family circles have reunions, round tables create harmonious political circles, as King Arthur knew. Those with whom we surround ourselves are our circle of friends.

A ring is a circle. The wedding ring is the circle that means "with you I find my completeness." The circle of friends who join the wedded couple forms another concentric circle of completeness around them.

Ela and Leah, joining hands, form a circle, at the center of which is the heart. With body and with breath, they reiterate the circle of rivers and blood, of seasons and solar systems. On the Orbitone, they turn in circles; rolling Rainhoops, they play with circles. They are the center of a circle of friends. They are in the circle of intimates orbiting those friends. May their lives always be what the poet Rumi, clairvoyantly from the 13th century, said of them: "They turn as the sun and the moon turn, circling what they love."

Losing a Sunset in Arizona

As I drove through Ashland one spring day, I saw a flock of high school girls run down a side street to stand on Siskiyou Boulevard, waiting to cross the street. It was a beautiful early summer day, and one of the girls, too full of good spirits and high energy to stand in one place, was hopping crazily, teetering, jumping like a new lamb at play, as though the warm weather or some good news or maybe just an exuberance for life were more than she could bear. This was not a drug-induced high. Her joy was too sincere, her aspect too innocent, her companions too responsible. Her light blue jacket flew around her fashionably tight shirt and barely revealed belly button. In different clothes she could have been I decades ago.

Though I still feel the adult version of this emotion, I recognized in this girl that particular relevance of it to youth. But we come from youth to maturity by making mistakes, and if this innocent joy reflects youth's free spirit, youth's susceptibility to flattery reflects the demise of that innocence. As I drove past the girls on the sidewalk, I remembered once when I myself, in my youth, spoiled a moment of unconditional joy because I was flattered by a man.

I was in Arizona during the early '70s, the hippie era, for a healing gathering at a hot springs. On this particular evening I emerged from a long soak in the spa to witness a glorious desert sunset. Blazing Arizona rocks snatched fire from the sky. Flaming arrows of gold shot from roiling cloud mountains. Scarlet challenged orange. Orange burst through magenta. Magenta enveloped rose. Rose swallowed scarlet.

In the joy of that moment I knew only one possible response: to run fast enough to catch this sunset. I had to pound the earth with my bare feet and fly through the wind to feel my hair streaming behind me and my face keeping pulse with the glowing sky. As I ran, Gerard Manley Hopkins whispered in my ear through the wind: "How to keep is there any such any bow or brooch or clasp or key to keep keep keep this beauty from fading away?" Yes – run. Catch it, keep it as long as possible by running west, towards the sunset. I would keep it beauty beauty beauty from fading away with the freedom of this run.

A suave, musical male voice spoke to me.

"Hello, Diana."

I knew that voice. To say that the man it belonged to was the most popular man at the healing gathering would be an understatement. He was the stereotype of stardom, his attractiveness the cliché of good looks, and he carried with him that insolence of the cocky male ego that implied he could have whatever he wanted. I didn't really care for him, but he had never paid much attention to me, and my disdain was a cover for the sting of his insult. And now he had called my name. He had deigned to admit me to the status of the worthy and to honor me with his blue-eyed attention.

I stopped. I turned. I gave him a big smile, and in the glass of his eyes I saw my sunset, beauty, beauty, beauty, fade away. Along with the sunset faded that moment of wild, free exuberance in my soul.

To Him Who Would Have Me Stint My Vocabulary for the Sake of Bears with Very Little Brain

"I am a Bear of Very Little Brain," says Winnie the Pooh, tugging at my shirttail, "and long words Bother me."

But, Pooh, I am a bear of, well, medium-sized brain, and I love words of all sizes: long ones like *apotheosis*, short words like *eat*, *sleep*, and *love*, fat ones like *crwth* and *thwart*, tall ones like *diddle a little*, onomatopoeic ones like *ping-pong*, and obscure ones like *obfuscate*, as long as I don't obfuscate my meaning when I say that words are the apotheosis of the language.

Should I stint such beauty? Should I trade preciseness for carelessness, exultation for mundanity, the music of words for a dull, plodding procession of overused syllables? No. As a lingophile, I have an obligation to use the words in my treasury lest they atrophy from the body of my language. If those of us who know them don't use them, they might end up on the linguistic Threatened and Endangered List. If an archaic word is one retired from active use, an obsolete word is extinct. I mourn when I find an obsolete word of great beauty – *lirepoop*, for instance, something to be learned as a lesson. What a shame not to be able to say to the children any more, "Come, children, it's time for your lirepoop." Or to call a slatternly woman *dawish*, to say I want to *finify* myself when I put on earrings, or to praise a husband for being a good *getpenny*. Alas, these words have gone the way of the saber-toothed tiger and the wooly mammoth.

Besides, Pooh, it isn't the size of the word that counts. It's the use. Even short words can make obscure statements, as witness the incomprehensibly ornate prose of Thomas Hobbes: "When a man reasoneth, he does nothing else but conceive a sum total, from addition of parcels, or conceive a remainder, from subtraction of one sum from another; which, if it be done by words, is conceiving of the consequence of the names of all the parts, to the name of the whole." On the other hand, Shakespeare creates grace and clarity from any sized word: "Absent thee from felicity awhile/And in this harsh world draw thy breath in pain/To tell my story."

Of course, we don't want to go around sounding like Shakespeare all the time, even if we could. "Put this in your pipe and smoke it" might make the same point. The vocabulary must serve the occasion. Shakespeare himself knew well the error of pompous language. In *Love's Labours Lost*, Don Armado says he will meet the princess "in the posteriors of this day, which the rude multitude call the afternoon." Such vocabulary was the "taffeta phrases, silken terms precise" and "figures pedantical" that Don Armado terms the "summer flies" that have "blown him full of maggot ostentation." He had to get rid of them before he could marry the princess.

Nabokov's vocabulary leaves me miles behind, yet it isn't full of maggot ostentation, and I relish his words. But if we don't want to sound like Shakespeare or Nabokov, we also don't want to sound like Huckleberry Finn: "But that's always the way," Huck says, "it don't make no difference whether you do right or wrong, a person's conscience ain't got no sense, and just goes for him anyway." Well, you could hardly have said it better than Huckleberry, but only if you were Huckleberry.

The larger the vocabulary, the more precision, beauty, and clarity possible for linguistic sculptures. Latinate words can embellish the language while Anglo-Saxon words keep it firmly grounded. I seek not to weaken my vocabulary by stinting it for the sake of Pooh-bears but to strengthen it, not to lay it aside but to exercise it, not to obscure my writing but to hone it into beauty and sense. Come, Pooh, I know you agree. Let me put it in your terms. If you had 2500 kinds of honey before you, you would use them all, wouldn't you?

The Bear Knew

The day before I was to leave for Greece, I woke up with a migraine hovering. I managed to teach the class at Southern Oregon University where I was the invited guest lecturer, but then I crumpled under the headache and spent the night with a friend in Ashland. The headache was gone the next morning, and I left Ashland early to go home, finish packing, and do everything necessary to be gone for a month. I left home around noon, a tad late but not too bad. I had things to do in Grants Pass but was on the freeway headed for Portland by early afternoon, in good time to visit my friends there that evening, as planned. I had to be at the airport by 11:00 the next morning.

About 40 miles north of Eugene, where I had stopped for lunch, it occurred to me I hadn't seen my ticket in my pocketbook when I paid for lunch. As I drove, I visualized every item in my pocketbook and found no ticket. I visualized my carryon pack and found no ticket. Increasingly anxious, I visualized my suitcase, too, but I knew my ticket wasn't there. As soon as I could, I pulled off the freeway and, with a sinking heart, did the actual searches that I knew correctly would reveal no ticket. I didn't waste a minute with recriminations. I could excoriate myself while driving. I turned around and headed towards home, trying frantically to visualize where the ticket might be.

There were plenty of recriminations. I was humiliated at my carelessness with a ticket my friends in Sweden had paid for. I was embarrassed and disappointed that I had spoiled the visit with my friends in Portland. I was terrified I wouldn't find the ticket when I got home. And I certainly didn't want to get into an accident, because I could hear my friends saying, in puzzlement, "But what was she doing driving south?"

I got home around 6:30. After a great search, I finally found my ticket. I called my friends in Portland to apologize.

Then I made cookies to take to my friends in Sweden and went to bed. Everything was all right. I would have to leave at 5:00 in the morning to get to the airport by 11:00, but I could do it.

At 1:00 a.m. I awoke to an awful banging and clanging in the back yard. Grabbing my flashlight, I flew down the ladder and out the back door. In the yard was a bear, tearing into a garbage bag. I chased him through the woods, yelling. I stopped. He stopped, so I chased him again, yelling. He ran, then stopped. I chased, yelled, stopped, chased some more until he was deep in the woods. Then I came back and picked up the garbage he had strewn over the yard, double bagged it, and carried it down the hill to a shed. Back at the house, I picked up the compost bucket he had knocked over but couldn't open. I washed away its odiferous spilled juices with a hose. Because I was doing some construction on my house, my back door was only propped in place, looking closed but actually not even on its hinges. I now saw that I was being careless. A bear could just give it a little shove and walk right in. So, working by flashlight (I live too deep in the woods for electrical lines), I found the hinges, did a little banging with the hammer, and rehung the back door. I put a lock on it. I went around the house locking all the doors. I plugged up my cat door and gave the cats an open window upstairs. Finally, I went to bed for the remaining hours. I left at 5:00, my ticket firmly in my pocket. I got to the airport by 11:00 and was safely on the plane when it took off.

And do you know what? I think that bear had it all figured out. He knew I was going to be gone that night. Well, I fooled him, didn't I?

Patches

When I was a little girl, my sister Linda and I were both horse-crazy. We read horse books, collected horse statues, and spent hours drawing horses – horses grazing in pastures, galloping with folded legs, trotting with pricked ears. A horse of our own was beyond family means, but one summer our parents agreed to board a neighbor's horse while that family vacationed.

He was a big gray Tennessee Walker named Patches, good-tempered, with a beautiful rolling gait, easy to ride in spite of his size. Linda and I fed Patches in the newly fenced paddock, kept his water trough full, and groomed him to perfection. I loved to rub my hands over his sleek neck, kiss his nose, breathe his good strong horsy smell.

A young girl, Shirley, came to the house weekly to give us riding lessons. She taught us to walk and trot Patches on the graveled driveway circling the well before allowing us the longer ride up the driveway and back. The first time one of us – Linda – rode Patches to the top of the driveway, though, he smelled home – his real home – and, ignoring Linda's increasingly hysterical cries of "Whoa!" and manipulations of the reins, he galloped for the old corral with the instinct of a migrating goose and the pace of an equine star in an old Western. My mother was beside herself with worry. I thought she was overreacting and said to comfort her, "But we know where he's going."

Apparently getting lost wasn't a concern. "What if she falls off!" my mother wailed.

Oh. I hadn't thought about that. Then I began to worry, too.

We found Patches, as expected, panting next to his old barn, Linda still safely astride. The next several times Linda or I rode Patches to the top of the driveway, he would stubbornly stop, his ears pricked, longing to run to his old home but knowing he shouldn't. Shirley would break a limber branch off a sweet-gum tree and walk up the long hill to the stalled horse and rider. Shirley would hand the switch to the rider, telling her to tighten the reins and squeeze her knees, then hit Patches smartly on the rump. When we did, he took off with a jerk, but we held on. Control of a horse is a good thing to learn.

We also learned how to lay a saddle on Patches's back and how to outfox him by waiting to tighten the cinch till he deflated his belly. We learned how to pull a bridle over his nose, forcing the bit between his big yellow teeth and folding his ears through the top leather pieces, straightening and stroking the long silky ears afterwards. Docilely, patiently Patches accepted these attentions while our collie, Rusty, wound through the long equine legs in excitement. When we went for a ride, Rusty loped alongside till he was left behind. When we returned, he ran to meet us.

Patches was a good horse, but we had been warned about one eccentricity: he didn't like to be petted while he ate. One day, when I brought him his hay, I disregarded the warning. He had always liked my petting and had never been mean, so I stayed to stroke his neck, pat his withers, and lovingly untangle his mane with my fingers. Suddenly he put back his ears and rushed at me, his eyes roaring, "Don't do that!" To make his point even more clear, he bit me on the arm.

I screamed and cried. Rusty was beside himself with worry, wiggling, whining, and jumping. Patches tranquilly returned to his dinner. Mom rushed from the house. While she bandaged my arm and Rusty thrust his nose into the doctoring scene, I begged her not to tell Dad. I knew I was to blame, not Patches. Mom said we ought to tell Dad how heroically Rusty had behaved. I didn't care. I wasn't afraid of punishment, but I was ashamed of having disobeyed.

Of course, she told him. Adult now, I understand why. Dad must have thought it wasn't necessary to expose my shame or Mom's betrayal of my wishes because he never mentioned the incident. It was I who brought it up more than 40 years later while he and Mom and I were having a glass of his homemade quince wine. When I told this story, we all had a good laugh. It's the kind of story you can laugh about when you're an adult.

"I loved Patches," I said. "I was always so grateful for having had him."

"Taking care of a horse sure got rid of your craving to have your own," Mom said with the hint of a sneer. "We never heard another word from you or Linda about wanting a horse after that summer."

I took a sip of wine, then spoke carefully. "Did you think that caring for a horse was so much trouble I was cured of wanting one? But that wasn't true! I didn't beg for a horse any more because I knew we couldn't afford one. Dad had promised Linda and me a horse, and he had kept his promise. That's why."

Mom gave a simpering chuckle. Dad picked up the newspaper. The conversation was over, but I have pondered ever since how we can draw the wrong conclusions from the most straightforward facts and events. In the case of Patches, the misconception had no important consequences, but many serious quarrels and conflicts – between lovers, between neighbors, between heads of state – must be based on deeply hidden and undiscovered false interpretations of facts.

The Thing I Feared the Most Has Come To Pass

I came home one evening to find the kind of message on my telephone that we all dread, but that we know will come at one time or another: "Mom had a stoke this morning. She's paralyzed on her right side. She can't move her arm and can't talk."

My mother, my vital, energetic mother, who, even at 87, was always painting and still teaching classes, who drove herself to church every Sunday in her Le Baron convertible, the good hostess, the beloved teacher, the darling of all who knew her – this feisty woman now unable to hold a paintbrush or walk through her flower beds or talk? It seemed inconceivable, but it wasn't. Both her father and her mother had suffered debilitating strokes. Now I could imagine my mother thinking, "That which I have feared the most has come to pass."

For weeks I felt helpless and useless and far away. My three sisters in Atlanta were with Mom day and night. They held her in their arms while she cried, cheered her when she felt discouraged, and strained to understand what she wanted: I want to go outside; the crooked picture on the wall is bugging me; a funny thing happened with the nurse yesterday. They urged her to feed herself with her left hand and praised her when at last she was able to twitch her right shoulder. They combed her hair and gave her sponge baths and brought her flowers and cards and good wishes from scores of friends. They wrote down for her, as she made it clear she wanted, the name of every person who came to see her, sent a card, called, or brought food to the house, where, I understood, the refrigerator was overflowing.

My daily phone calls, my daily cards seemed insignificant in the face of what my sisters were doing. I asked a hundred questions: "How's her progress?" "How's her spirit?" "What do the doctors say?" I followed each incremental improvement: the day she walked by herself with a four-pronged cane, the day she was taken on an excursion through the hospital garden, the day she said her first intelligible words, "Thank you," to the nurse for making her bed. I was told how angry she was for the first few days, angry just to be in this condition, how frustrated she got at not being able to talk and how amazingly well she communicated anyway, how much she longed to drive past her house when she was moved to the rehabilitation center, how she charmed all the nurses, how everyone marveled at the way she faced her situation with spirit and intelligence. Dad was with her every day. When I asked about his and Mom's relationship (not always exemplary these past few years), my sister told me, "It's heartrendingly tender. It's so sweet it would break your heart."

Almost a month after the stroke, I flew to Georgia to be with Mom when she came home from the rehabilitation center, for that was the time, my sisters and I had agreed, I would be most useful. I gave my sisters some relief, allowing them to return to more normal life while I interrupted mine, as they had theirs, to take advantage of the opportunity to repay Mom, a little, for all she has done for us. While I was there, I was watching her to learn all I could because it is entirely possible that the genetic strain that brought my mother to this point lies in me as well, and if, some day, I find myself saying, "That which I have feared the most has come to pass," I hope I can face it with resilience and determination, that I will have learned from my mother how best to do it.

A New "Adopted Daughter" for My Mother

After my mother's stroke, the family had to find a full-time caregiver for her, but my mother fought hard against the idea of a caregiver. She didn't want a stranger living in the house. She thought I should move back to Atlanta and take the job (impossible thought!). Inevitably we had to hire a stranger. We told the hiring agency we didn't need an RN, but someone who could handle a medical emergency, drive a car, do light housework, laundry, cooking – someone who would be competent, reliable, friendly (but not intrusive), respectful of privacy (but always ready to help), and available 24 hours a day. I doubted that anyone could do this job, but I didn't say anything. We tried to comfort Mom by suggesting this person might turn into an adopted daughter, a designation for a handful of younger women who have become like daughters to her. Mom just sneered.

Then Janice arrived. My sisters told me she was a Godsend, interesting, intelligent, and pleasant. She has the rudimentary medical understanding for basic nursing needs and handles medical emergencies with practiced calm. She sleeps near a monitor connected to Mom's bedside and gets up without complaint at any hour to help my mother, night after night, when she calls. As a result of the stroke Mom is often querulous and difficult, finding fault in the smallest thing and turning hysterical when things go awry. Janice reasons gently with her, tries to understand the problem, speaks soothingly. She is a 'round-the-clock caregiver for my mother, but she keeps an eye on my 96-year-old father, too. She deals with the idiosyncrasies of diet and taste between my mother and my father, handles the complicated regime of my mother's medications, keeps track of doctors' and therapists' appointments, and drives Mom to these appointments. She seems to be always aware of what needs to be done, whether it's a load of laundry or a haircut for my mother. If she has a few minutes, she does some ironing or sweeps the kitchen. Sometimes, in the evening, for a break, she'll watch television. She gets tired, as any of us do at any job, but after a weekend off, she returns with grace and eagerness.

When I was in Georgia last month to visit my parents, my mother was in the hospital again, so I met Janice at the house, on my own. I liked her at once, but it wasn't until I saw her with my mother that I understood the depth of her value as a caregiver. When Janice, Dad, and I walked into Mom's hospital room, Mom pointed to Janice and said, "She's wonderful!" Janice pointed her finger right back at my mother and said, "You're wonderful!" Mom reached for Janice's hand, drew her to her bedside, turned to me, and said, "This is one of my adopted daughters."

Southpaw Art

As soon as my mother got home from the hospital after her stroke last April, one of her former tole painting students, determined that Mom not stop painting, brought her an easel. My sister Laura gave her a box of pastels. Gradually, 87 years old and handicapped by her stroke, she began to paint again. Even though apraxia kept her from being able to write or even to wave or point accurately, somehow when the left hand was asked to paint, the right side of the brain took over. The large pad of paper on my mother's easel grew fat with finished pastel paintings. They were amazingly good, and one day Laura broached an idea: Mom should have a show of left-handed paintings, to be held the last Sunday in March, when both my brother and I would be there.

The idea sustained my mother for weeks. The show would be called "An Art-full Life" (in spite of Dad's suggestion of "Southpaw Art"). When I arrived at my parents' house, I found paintings all over the house, mostly florals, a few land-scapes – a large magnolia blossom in a metal frame, a small close-up of two daffodils, the lenten rose in several variations, an Irish castle, a landscape of mountains and wildflowers. Many pictures had already sold. Unframed paintings littered flat sur-faces. For days my mother wandered from one pile to another, rearranging pictures, correcting lines, selecting pieces for me to take to my father to frame in his shop or to the framers in Sandy Springs. Every once in a while she started a new picture. "Somebody stop that woman!" my sister cried, keeping tabs on expenses. But no one wanted to stop her.

In the shop I found my 97-year-old father leaning over a cluttered table, meticulously measuring and remeasuring every cut, bearing down on the mat knife with such knotted hands I was sure the knife would slip past the marked stop. It never did.

Projects in progress lay untouched around him. Sawdust lay thick on the floor. The desk was littered with scraps of paper flecked with measurements and diagrams. "I don't have time to clean up," he told me, shoving aside a piece of wood with his foot, raising a small cloud of sawdust.

The show was a marvelous success. A hundred people came. Old friends, friends from Mom's church, family members, and former students crowded the gallery, congratulating Mom and Dad, telling them what a wonderful occasion this was. With each person who came in, my mother rasped, "Oh, good!" – her way of saying how glad she was to see that particular person. Guests wandered around the gallery, drinking my father's homemade wine and admiring the art – Mom's paintings and Dad's turned wooden bowls, also on display. At an appropriate time during the show, Laura made an announcement: the five Coogle children had started a Ken and Lois Coogle Art Scholarship Fund to continue our parents' legacy of art by ensuring art education for children in Sandy Springs.

That all the paintings sold and that the scholarship fund swelled immediately were significant honors, but I didn't know about the greatest tribute till that night as I was helping Mom into bed. She looked up at me and said, with a touch of wonder in her voice, "They asked me to teach a class in pastels."

Selling Picasso

I wandered for hours through the Göteborg Art Museum's fine collection of Nordic paintings – Carl Larsson's self-portrait, a very Munchian Edvard Munch, the beautiful *Nordic Summer Evening* by Richard Bergh, the bright sea and sunset colors of Carl Kylberg. I walked through rooms of paintings depicting the "Northern light" period of Nordic art, the Göteborg colorists, the humorous drawings of Arsenius, and into the room of the museum's small collection of modern French art. There, *The Acrobat's Family,* by Picasso, arrested my step.

With apologies to all the Scandinavian artists I had been viewing for hours, I had to admit that this painting was startlingly, forcibly beautiful. It contained that incomparable Picasso line – confident, sure, clean, strong, commanding. With that line and some soft paints, we see the acrobat's family: the acrobat in his circus costume, standing, and his wife, sitting, with their child in her lap, her hands holding the baby delicately, with just the fingertips. Both the baby and the mother are animated with spirit. Warm affection emanates from the father. Strangely, in the forefront of the picture sits a baboon, his back to us as he gently gazes at the mother and child. The picture is hauntingly beautiful with some tenderness that can't be accounted for by line and paint. The power of the picture is more than its subject matter, more than its style or its line and color. The power of the picture is in its genius.

A few days earlier, standing with me before this painting, my Swedish friend Lasse had told me there had been a suggestion that Göteborg sell *The Acrobat's Family.* "Göteborg is in financial straits," he explained.

"Yes," I said ironically, thinking of the Sierra Club's proposal to sell Clair Tappan Lodge, Rogue Community College selling its trees, the stories of people selling family heirlooms.

"That's what we do when we see red in the ledger – we sell our assets."

"This painting is worth millions of dollars," Lasse pointed out.

"But it's the same old argument: the arts have no intrinsic value. Arts programs are the first to go when schools pinch pennies."

"We need the money for social programs, help for children."

"Your art students need Picasso. They need this painting."

"We don't have enough Picassos here to be significant to our art students. They have easy access to Paris museums, anyway, with their much better collections."

My arguments, though not my convictions, were weakening. "It's an interesting debate," I admitted, "but the need for money makes us do regrettable things."

As we turned away, Lasse told me that in the end the debate in the city had been largely academic, since the painting had been a gift to the city and couldn't be sold.

Now, standing again in front of *The Acrobat's Family*, I knew in my bones that to lose this picture would be to impoverish Göteborg, whatever the city might have done with the money.

A"B"-line for Beatitude

When Ela and Leah were planning their wedding, they asked for "pearls of wisdom" from family and friends about relationships. This is the advice I sent them:

Begin with blessings. Every morning, every meeting: "I love you. You are my happiness. Bless you for being." Then carry on.

Build bridges. When the waters grow turbulent between you, stop a moment, take a step back, and consider how you might build a bridge on which the two of you may meet. You'll be surprised at how quickly it can be done.

Belittle your battles. They're not nearly so important as they might seem.

Bumble through the brambles; break through the briars. Whether you are bumbling or bursting through your forest of difficulties, know always there is a way to the other side.

Butter up the bitter. Things bitter to take will inevitably come your way, so just do the best you can with them. Butter them up to make them easier to take, and digest them well.

Banter away the blues. Laugh together to keep the sun shining.

Banish busy, leaving space to fill with love.

Bring bountiful baubles to each other: a book, a bagel, a bead, a bracelet, a belt, a bangle, a bone, or a bud; a leaf, a rock, a feather, or a shell set in a box, a bowl, a bag, a basket, a bundle, or a bin. Bring bouquets and bonbons or the story of a spider web broidered on a rose. Whatever they are, bring bountiful baubles to say, "I love you."

Bear bungles bravely. You will make mistakes, with each other and in life's circumstances. So square your shoulders and admit you bungled or smile wanly at the bungle of the other. Accept the inevitable human frailty of yourselves and carry on.

Bond with biscuits. That is to say, eat together. Sharing good food feeds the relationship as well as the body.

Bewitch your beloved. The birds and the bees are important.

Butterflies and bears, beetles and bees and birds and birches, bugs and beasts of all kinds are also important. Be in nature together. It gives you a larger context for yourselves and your relationship.

Behold the beauty of your belle or of your beau, and never, ever, ever neglect to say it's so.

Befriend your belle and your beau. Don't forget to be friends to each other, learning how to banish busy and belittle battles to do so.

Finally, bask in being blessed and believe your bliss. It's right there in front of you – next to you in bed, across from you at the dinner table, in your hand and in your arms – for the rest of your life. Always, always, always recognize the blessing and believe in your happiness. It's a gift given to you. It's the gift you give each other. Bask in blessings and believe your bliss. It's a beeline to beatitude.

Dad's Thumb

"And yet he hadde a thumb of gold," Chaucer said about his Miller, meaning that he increased his income by pressing his thumb on the scale as he weighed the flour. We all know what a green thumb is, and a black thumb is the carpenter's nemesis, but my father's thumbs might most suitably be identified by Macbeth's witches: "By the pricking of my thumbs/Something wicked this way comes."

When I was a child, my father cut off the end of his left thumb on a table saw as he was making the family dining table. His thumb was bound to his stomach for weeks for the skin graft. Ever since then his left thumb has had a discolored, slanted tip to it.

This spring as my father was working in his shop, a drill bit fell and sliced off the tip of his right thumb. There was no need for a skin graft this time, but oh, how the opposable thumb seemed to be opposing my father! And how sympathetic the family was to the plight of a man harried and hounded by thumb misfortune.

My sister Laura sent him a postcard from Florida. "Let me give you a thumbnail sketch of our trip," she said. "(Oh, sorry, Dad.) Unfortunately, I was all thumbs on the putting green but managed to have a good round anyway. Just visited Leu Botanical Garden – beautiful – obviously some green thumbs there! But no daphnes – guess I can thumb my nose at them about that! Had great shrimp last night that were about as big around as – you guessed – my thumb!"

As for me, I told my father I felt so sorry for him, laid up with injury as he was, with nothing to do but sit around and twiddle his thumbs.

Actually, though, I can think of a number of things for such a thumb-struck man to do. He could thumb through the pages of a magazine. He could take up the thumb piano for artistic expression. He could buy plum pies and stick his thumb in them in the hopes of pulling out a plum of a land deal, as Jack Horner did for the bishop of the Church of England. He could take up hitchhiking, thumbing rides all over the country but avoiding places where he might stick out like a sore thumb. And he could advise everyone that the rule of thumb – that the rod with which to beat the wife should be no bigger than the thumb – went out with wifebeating.

Oh, I'm sorry. It seems mean to tease a man about his thumb misfortunes, but my father is a good sport and enjoys a pun as much as the rest of us, so I'll let him have the last word. "Dear Thumbalina," he wrote back to Laura. "Thumbtimes when you thumb your nose at thumbthing thumbbody has done, thumbhow the thumb of your efforts reaches the thumbmit of the ridiculous. If thumb thumbmer day you thumb a ride to thumbwhere, you may be thumberstruck at the thumbwhat less than thumbtuous results."

It sounds a little like it was the tip of Dad's tongue, not his thumb, that was cut off, but, I say, thumbs up! to my father on this Father's Day.

Poppies for My Grandmother

Even old age, says Dylan Thomas, should burn and rage at close of day. "Do not go gentle into that good night," he urges. But before her death my grandmother ached for the soft, blessed darkness.

She had already lived longer than she should. When my grandfather died, 13 years earlier, the burden of her life was as a half-filled vessel tediously borne. She grew older and older, suffered three strokes, and finally degenerated so badly her son and daughter took her to a nursing home. "You can't live by yourself any more," they said, knowing better than she what was good for her. "You might set the house on fire with a forgotten pot on the stove. This is a nice place. We'll come to visit as often as we ever did."

To help her bear this changed life, I began writing weekly letters. "Dear Grandma. It's spring here in the mountains of Oregon, and the plum tree is in bloom, reminding me of you and Grandpa and the farm in Kentucky," speaking now of my grandfather not only because I thought she would like to recall the days of summer but also in atonement for an injustice I have done her. For years her letters to me had inevitably ended in a pitiful, plaintive whine: "I miss your grandfather."

"Come on, Grandmother," I would think, "get on with the living. Be here now. Accept what is." But my youthful vigor was callous, my illusory perspicacity a gross injustice to the habits and feelings of half a century of marriage I could know nothing of, either then or now.

To atone for that guilt and to deflect the possibility of another I wrote to her, but I was writing into a responseless void, and when the time came that she no longer recognized my mother, I stopped writing. If she didn't know the voice and face of the daughter, how could she know the granddaughter by the written word? Her periods of nonlucidity grew stronger, leaving ever briefer moments of recognition. "The nurse came into the room," my mother told me, "and found her under the bed."

"She doesn't even know she's alive," my sister said. If she had not been spoon-fed three times a day with institutional regularity, she would simply have stopped eating, not with the volition to kill herself, but passively, longing to go gentle into that good night.

I had a friend once whose longing was less passive, not so much to meet the night as to escape the bright, harsh, unbearable day. He told me he was going to commit suicide soon, and all that awful week before he died, I tried to reach him in the limbo he inhabited between the living and the nonliving to tell him, somehow, "I love you," because soon it would be too late. We took a drive through the mountains together, but he was distant. I read a favorite poem to him one last time, but his politeness was no mask for his not caring. I picked a handful of wild poppies and wild lilacs and gave them to him where we rested on a hill overlooking the ocean. He slowly took them and looked at me with wonder and recognition of beauty, and I knew that he had returned at last to hear me say, "Farewell."

The last time I saw my grandmother was nine years ago. She was in the last apartment she would live in by herself, old, frail, and unable to care for herself properly, my mother said, dashing in to wash the dishes and vacuum the floor. "Your hair is a mess," she said, combing out the tangles in the weeks-ago beauty-parlor-curled mass of gray.

My grandmother looked at me and said, "I wish she would just sit down and visit."

So I did. "Show me your miniature pitcher collection," I said, and she did, her eyes magnified to predestined senility behind her glasses as, one by one, she picked up her miniature pitchers, pouring memories from this place and that, from one friend and another.

I was humbly grateful that one of the memory-full pitchers on my grandmother's shelf was from me because now it is too late to give her things she might enjoy. My grandmother died a few days later, old, senile to the point of madness, raging not against the dying of the light but against the continuation of the light, that bright artificial electric light bulb that wouldn't let her sleep when darkness had already closed around her. Her death has released for me fresher memories of a more vigorous woman than the one who died in the nursing home, and it has made me hope our last visit together was sufficient farewell because all that is left for me now is to lay these poppies in blessing on her grave.

101 Memories of Mom

For my mother's 85th birthday, my sister Laura made her a list of 85 memories. I was intrigued both with the list and with the exercise and decided I would do the same. I gave Mom my list of memories for Christmas. I'm sure she enjoyed reading them, but the value of the gift, I learned to my surprise, lay in the process.

I began by simply writing down the first memories that occurred, but I was startled and a little ashamed to discover that they were all unhappy ones, from the years during my 20s and 30s, my hippie years, when my mother didn't like the way I was living. I had to work through all of those dark memories before the brighter ones could percolate. The first of those were the easy memories, the ones I had brought into consciousness many times before – my mother walking out of the grocery store saying, "I spent $40! But grocery bills are cheaper than doctor bills," or my mother sending me pear branches in February to put in a jar of water in my dorm room at Vanderbilt University and force into pre-spring blossoms. Other easy memories were the collective family memories, like the one of my mother standing back every year after decorating the Christmas tree and saying, "It's the prettiest tree we've ever had!"

After that I had to work a little harder to remember things. In my memory I scanned particular events for my mother's involvement – family Christmases, summer visits to Grandpa's farm, our family trip to Alaska, times when I was hurt or injured. I began to be more and more discriminatory about what memories were acceptable for my list. They had to be more than general family memories but specific to my mother – not "family excursions to the Topples' cabin at Lake Lanier" but "my mother painting the glass door at the Topples' cabin at Lake Lanier." Sometimes I cheated and rewrote a memory so that it centered on her. My memory of the Norman Rockwell magazine covers on the wall by the basement stairs, for instance, became "You pasting *Saturday Evening Post* covers on the wall by the stairway to the basement."

In the end, I had a list of 101 memories I could stick in my mother's Christmas stocking. I wondered how many of them she, too, would recall, and I wondered how much she would learn about me by reading my memories. But the main value of those 101 memories lay in what I learned about her as I brought childhood memories into the light of adulthood. For instance, I remembered feeling sorry for my mother on our trip to Alaska as the rest of the family ran off to swim in a lake or explore the woods, leaving her alone in the campground, painting wildflowers at a picnic table. Now I think how she must have cherished those uninterrupted hours doing what she liked best to do. Like the rest of us, I complained about Spam sandwiches on that same trip, but now I realize how hard it was for her to plan meals along the Alcan, where supplies were scarce. Nor had I understood my mother as a woman who "enjoyed life to the hilt" (she was just my mother) until I saw how many memories included her good humor.

My father is not a sentimental person, and I'm not sure he would appreciate a list of memories as much as my mother, but I think I'll draw up such a list for him for his 96th birthday this March. The thing is, I'm not sure I'll be doing it for him or for me.

Lilliputian Advantages

Unless you are as short as I, you may have thought about the disadvantages of being five feet tall, but you may not have realized the advantages. Having to drag stools and ladders around the house to reach that vase or book on the top shelf probably doesn't surprise you, nor having the view of concerts, plays, and parades blocked by heads, hats, and hair, but maybe you haven't realized that being so short I am even more claustrophobically confined in crowds than the average person – crushed, for instance, between big chests and muscled arms in a crowd of Russians, who pack more tightly than Americans. But I have an advantage in crowds, too, because I can slip under elbows and around hips as quick and lithe as a weasel or a child.

Although I feel compelled to offer the front seat in compact cars to my longer-legged companions, the sacrifice is more visual than tactile. On planes and buses I am less cramped than they, and if I am lucky enough to have an empty seat next to me on an overnight trip, I can lie horizontally and sleep comfortably enough. In planes, if I have to struggle till someone takes pity and helps me pull my luggage from the furthest reaches of the overhead compartments, I have already received compensation for that difficulty: as soon as the plane comes to a complete stop and passengers can stand, I immediately stand upright, even if I am in a window seat. I stretch gratefully while all around me the unfortunate taller passengers are crunching their heads into their necks against the overhead compartments as we all wait interminably to disembark.

Being elf-sized, I am used to tilting my head back, looking into nostrils, when talking to people. This stance is so normal that when I address someone my height or, rarely, even shorter, I feel awkward and gawky, as though I tower and loom. Of course, it's different with children, though by the time most children are adolescents, it's they who feel awkward, exclaiming, "You're so short!"

I am constantly aware of living in a world made for taller people. When I try on dresses, the hems drag on the floor. Sometimes I find better fits in the children's department. That's where I found my rubber boots. Never mind that they had chartreuse trim; at least they weren't imprinted with teddy bears. When I sit at meetings or concerts, my feet swing above the floor, so I hook them around chair rungs or tuck them under me. When I lecture, I feel hidden behind a lectern, so I sidestep it. To feel visible at the counters of banks and post offices, I stand on tiptoes. Sometimes, at restaurants or in friends' homes, I can't quite reach the table without uncomfortably lifting my arms, though I stop short of asking for a dictionary to sit on.

Hugging is awkward, especially if my reciprocal hugger is as tall as I am short. Standing uphill or on steps helps. Otherwise, I hug a lot of stomachs, or, in an attempt to match a man's height, I sort of clasp my wrists around his neck and stand on tiptoe while he crumples his body towards me, and we hug with a lot of air between us.

But do you know what? If someone were to offer to increase my height by four or five inches, I'd say no, thanks. I like the Lilliputian advantages.

Old Violins Sing Beauty, but Old Bread Is Best Thrown Out

An old car thunks and rattles and hums throatily. The cab smells like bare wet metal, the upholstery like 200,000 miles of bottoms and backs.

An old house creaks and leaks. It smells like decades of cookies, dusty corners, and patient wood. At its sagging joints, the air squeezes in.

Old rugs carry the history of feet.

Old glass ripples like a brook, distorting with Methuselah speed the fresh, clear image of its youth.

Old photographs in discolored tones retain that fresh, clear image: Mom smiling under her '40s hairdo at her first-born babe, Dad still in his black mustache and Navy uniform.

Old clothes grow sheer and spare. The white silk blouse thins to shreds across the shoulder; the blue jeans tear at the knee and are patched, tear in the seat and are patched, tear at the other knee and are patched into a quilt of colorful squares on the legs of the young hippie girl in the old photograph.

Old T-shirts grow soft like a second skin. Old slippers and Birkenstocks mold to the feet (old shoes are easiest on the feet, said King James, who was in the habit of asking for his). Old hiking boots, having walked all those miles, become so trustworthy that in case of fire they would be saved first, along with the guitar and the computer.

Old tennis shoes resent their beating, tear at the seams where the toes spread, wear through the sole where the foot bears down at the twist of the serve, split at the tongue for having been impatiently pulled and tugged too often.

Old tennis shoes smell like the seats under the balcony of a French movie theater. They are probably dead long before they are thrown out.

Old cotton sheets wear to the transparency of onion skin. If they are half polyester, they lose the cotton and retain the polyester till one morning you wake up thinking, "I am sleeping on plastic."

Old sleeping bags have holes, as do old roads. In both cases, they're losing their stuffing.

Old lamps, old wooden chests, old cane-back chairs (restored), old china, old pottery, and old paintings of Old Masters are cherished because they are beautiful and rare, full of the mystery and sensitivity of history. They are best when the history is Grandma's and Great-grandma's.

Old violins, well bowed, sing beauty.

Old music is cherished for our memories locked therein, and it's the same with old people.

Old rocks are cherished for encoding the memories of the earth.

Old wood burns best.

Old wine is best to drink. Old bread is best thrown out.

"Old women," my grandmother said, "have trouble pulling on their panty hose." I think of these words every morning as I do yoga.

Old lovers are better in memory than they were at the time, and old friends are the dearest and truest friends of all.

The good old times, Lord Byron said, are gone. "All times when old are good," he said.

Old books are well thumbed from frequent openings, water-warped from bathtubs, and spotted with spaghetti sauce from dinners. They are well loved because they contain all the human condition, the echo of laughter, the tug at the heart, and all our fondness for the magic of words.

The old moon in the new moon's arms – ethereal, lucent, diaphanous as gossamer – is a likely home for Alexander Pope's sylphs, who have "fluid bodies half dissolved in light,/Thin glittering textures of the filmy dew."

Old trees are some of the most venerable beings on earth. So might we be, too, when we are old.

What's in a Name?

When Romeo was wooing Juliette and Juliette languishing in love for Romeo, she wished at first he had some other name. Then she decided it didn't matter. "What's in a name?" she said. "That which we call a rose/By any other name would smell as sweet."

But, Juliette, I don't think so. Connotations and phonics could very well influence how we perceive a smell. What if the rose were called – well, strumphbuggelwort? Would it still smell as sweet? Without pretty pinks and hints of the rosary, without the sweet long "o" drawn out by the "s," without the rhyme of Romeo's rose, how could a strumphbuggelwort smell as sweet as a rose? Could the yellow rose of Texas be the only strumphbuggelwort for me?

Names do signify, and naming is an important if not a sacred task. My son is Ela. He was born in a log cabin on the Cherokee Indian Reservation of North Carolina, where the Oconoluftee and Tuckaseegee Rivers come together at a small dam called Ela. Rather than calling him Oconoluftee or Tuckaseegee, his father and I decided on the simpler and more handsome name "Ela." Would Ela be as sweet if he were Oconoluftee instead? He says not.

Naming children Patience and Prudence, popular among the Puritans, has fallen from favor, perhaps because those qualities are no longer revered but probably more because it's no longer fashionable to mold personalities in that manner. If Patience is going to have a temper, either call her Patty or take responsibility for a split personality. If you name your son Romeo, he had better be good-looking, or you're responsible for the laughs. In Flannery O'Connor's story "Good Country People," Mrs. Hopewell names her daughter Joy. A bitter and vengeful girl, Joy later changes her name to Hulga – "the ugli-

116

est name in any language," asserts her resentful mother. A personality that refuses to be molded by the expectations of parents can defiantly prefer Hulga to Joy. The name is, at least, her own.

I once met a woman named Tennece (pronounced to rhyme with Denise). "That's a pretty name," I said. "Where did it come from?"

"My parents thought I was going to be a boy," she told me. "They had given him the name Tennel. When I turned out to be a girl, they feminized Tennel to Tennece."

Feminizing male names is not new. Consider "Roberta" from "Robert," "Denise" from "Dennis," "Carla" from "Carl." But masculinizing a girl's name is not done. There is no "Rebec" from "Rebecca" or "Lindus" from "Linda." Many old-fashioned boys' names that subsequently became unisex are now just girls' names: Shirley, Joyce, Carol. We can call a girl Bobbie or Johnny or Tommi, but heaven help the man named Sue!

Tennece told me her name had always given her trouble. People ask how to spell it and confuse it with Tennessee. She seemed vexed by this problem of her name but said, with a little smile, "What can I do? It's my name."

In the '70s people of my generation with names like John and Judy refused to say, "What can I do? It's my name." Despising the ordinary as symbols of the establishment, they sloughed their old names and took on new ones. Away with Jeff. Hello, Nataka. Good-bye, Katie. Hello, Arupa. Anna became Karima; David, Running Deer. Many a Hulga, no doubt, became Joy. Jade was named after a stone, Willow after a tree, and Mushroom after a fungus. I even met a man who, whatever the name he had been born with, was now called – appropriately – Grunge.

Childhood names can stick like glue. "Taffy" was cute at the age of five, but after her fourth child, the grown woman wanted to shed the nickname at last for the preferred given name Stephanie. Friends and family were less ready. How does Bobby finally become Robert? If Timothy changes "Mommy" to "Mom," why can't she stop calling him Timmy?

Last names, too, were sometimes changed – Funk to Eagleson, for instance. But it's a pity to lose our surnames because they tell us of our ancestors: the places they came from – Brownstone, Hill, Green; their occupations – Smith, Brewster, Farmer; their attributes – Short, Strong, White, Young. We can sense the tales in a name like Lawless, and we can understand why, although the telephone book shows many Weavers, Taylors, and Bakers – occupations, traditionally, of men – it lists no Spinsters.

I have always liked my name, both for its sound and for its meaning. The sound is rhythmic and rich, with the "a" on the end like a joyous exclamation point, far different from the nasal whine and plaintive wail of the e-on-the-end version, Diane. I detest being called "Diane." I try not to snap too viciously when I correct people who make that mistake, but I've noticed they usually rear back as though struck, unconsciously raising a hand, palm forward, taking a step backwards, saying, "Yes. *Diana*," thinking, "God help me, I'll never make that mistake again!"

Diana, or Artemis in Greek, was goddess of the moon and of the hunt. I, Diana, hunt the music in the interstices of life; I hunt the moon cycles of my own moods. Shunning bright reds and yellows, I wrap myself in the purples, blues, and silvers of the moon. In the night garden I move among the perfumes of moonvine, datura, and nicotiana. Have I unconsciously molded myself to fit my name? Or did my parents by mysterious chance give me the name that fit? Would I be different as "Sylvia" or "Gloria"?

Diana was also the goddess of chastity, but here the correspondence ends. I am not like Daphne of Greek mythology, who dedicated herself to Diana and rejected all suitors, even Apollo, who, lustful and lovestruck god of the sun, poetry, and music, chased her through the woods. She cried to her father, a river god, to help her. Obligingly, he turned her into a laurel tree.

Apollo, brokenhearted, declared the laurel his sacred tree, so we give laurels to victors – even though Apollo was the loser in the Daphne story.

Another name for Diana is Phoebe, since Artemis, the moon goddess, was the twin sister of Phoebus Apollo, the sun god. Yet another name is Selene, who was actually another moon goddess, and a fourth name is Cynthia from Diana's birthplace on Mt. Cynthus. In the lower world, Diana was known as "the dreaded Hecate of hell, mighty to shatter every stubborn thing," Hecate, the Goddess of the Dark of the Moon. So I could as easily have been called Cynthia or Selene or Phoebe, and, in my darker moments, when I seem "mighty to shatter every stubborn thing," or maybe just in my most mysterious inward moments or when I present an inscrutable face and cold demeanor, my friends think, "Ah, yes. She's in her Hecate phase. It'll pass."

If I Were To Call You Feline

Animals have given us many useful adjectives. For instance, if a dancer's movements are sleekly graceful and cat-like, we might call them *feline*. *Leonine*, lion-like, would imply something entirely different. George W. Bush is leonine in his greed, feline in his political maneuvers, and viperine (the meaning is obvious) in general. Being even more specific, or, perhaps, being viperine ourselves, we might also call him *thantophidian,* "like a poisonous snake." I myself would call him *bdelloid*, a word than means leech-like (think of his tax proposals). I would love to pronounce it as it's spelled, bringing the "b" out of its silence, but I won't because I don't want to be Bush-like (*Bushine*, maybe, or, taking our cue from another animal, *asinine*) in my language.

Most of us know equine recreation is horseback riding and that the canine unit of the police force is its dogs. If *orthopterous* were pronounced *ort-hop-terous,* we would surely see the grasshopper in it. Astrology buffs or any old hippie would understand that a *taurine* person is as stubborn as a bull (cf. Taurus) and that one who is *capric* is goat-like (as in Capricorn). If we know that *cameline* means "camel-like" and *pardine* (leaving off the leo) means "leopard-like," then *camelopardine* makes sense as the giraffe adjective, if you see giraffes as something like spotted camels. We might use the word to say that Botticelli painted a particularly camelopardine Aphrodite.

If you call me *vermilingual*, you don't mean I talk like a worm but that I have a worm-like tongue, though it's an adjective more appropriately applied to anteaters and chameleons. If I tell you that you're being absolutely *batoid* today, I don't mean that you're acting crazy. (The adjective for bat-like is the beautiful *vespertilian*, with its hint of evening.) By *batoid* I would mean you are as flat as a ray (the fish, not the sunbeam). You might throw an *apian* retort my way (with a bee-like sting to it) and tell me I'm pretty *edentate* myself. If I were Bushine (meaning, remember? Bush-like in my language skills), I might be flattered, thinking you meant "like Eden," whereas you were really telling me I was a sloth.

Linguistic traps like those in *batoid* and *edentate* lurk in many species adjectives. *Spermophiline* refers to the spermophile, a ground squirrel, and should not be confused with a *spermophiliac*, a nymphomaniac. To be *gadoid* doesn't mean "darting about like a gadfly" but "cod-like." Even though *urinatorial* refers to diving birds and comes from the Latin word meaning "to plunge under water," I would feel slightly uneasy if, as I surfaced from my dive, you told me, approvingly, I looked very urinatorial as I dove. Auditory associations overpower the etymology.

If you think I am being papilionaceous, "butterfly-like," with all this darting about from one word to another, I'll not be offended; *papilionaceous* is a beautiful word. Anyway, someone else may protest that this essay clarifies vocabulary and shines light on interesting words and etymologies, in which case he might call it *pellucid*, meaning "clear" – not to be confused with *pulicid*, "flea-like." At any rate it isn't my cygnine signature, my "swan song." There are many words yet to take wing as song.

The Dump, the Landfill, and the Transfer Station

When we took our garbage to the dump, we knew what we were doing with it – dumping it. But when the dump became a landfill, we thought we were doing something good for the land to give it our garbage, as though the land had a yearning, an emptiness, a great void that we could fill. Into the gaping mouth of the landfill we, mother birds, stuffed our nutrients. If the earth eats what is putrid and malodorous – dead animals decaying in the sun, rank and fetid compost, vegetables rotting in dark and stagnant water – then by classical logic the stench of the landfill proved the earth would eat our garbage. To aid in its digestion, huge bulldozers and backhoes, roaring and careening, mashed, crushed, and compacted the garbage, cramming it down the throat of the earth.

But the land can't eat what is indigestible, so it didn't swallow a lot of what we gave it, and after a while it could take no more, so we covered the mouth with more good earth, gave it a pat, and closed our eyes to its indigestion.

Now, the landfill having gone the way of the dump, we take our garbage, oh so cleanly, to the transfer site. Here there is no yawning maw to swallow the garbage but only a large concrete building with a concrete floor and windows that give light but no view. The land is not present. We take our garbage from the back of the car or the truck and toss it onto the concrete floor with a smack and a little flurry of dust. The place smells like a dump, it's true, and with the reverberating roar of heavy machinery, it sounds like a dump, and because what we do is dump and run, it feels like a dump, but the shift of image from landfill to transfer station is even greater than that from dump to landfill. The landfill, with the hugeness of its hole in the ground and the blink of an eye in which it was being filled, gave us a graphic sense of America's garbage problem. At the transfer station we see two dozen parking slots for that many vehicles to deposit that many dumps of garbage. Little piles of garbage sit around like bear dumps in the woods, and then a truck comes and scoops them away, and there is no more garbage and no problem.

Last week I made my annual dump run to the transfer station. Holding my breath against the stink, I flung my bulging, dirty, smelly black plastic bags of garbage from my car onto the concrete floor. I emptied my car's trash can. I considered throwing out my old tennis shoes, and I was tempted – oh, how I was tempted – to throw my car onto the heap and walk out of there on my own two feet, dusting my hands of all the garbage I owned and of all the garbage in America and of the whole garbage problem. But I kept my car and drove out of the garbage barn. As I turned my back on the concrete buildings, the staunch reality of what they contained nagged at me still, and before me hung the ultimate question of responsibility. If you put your garbage on the roadside for county or city services to pick up – whisk! it's gone. If you throw it onto the floor of the transfer station – whisk! it's gone. But, of course, it's not gone. It's just as present somewhere as it was in the landfill. I am afraid to ask where the garbage goes now, but I think that, unless we change our ways, it won't be long before we're like Shel Silverstein's Sarah Cynthia Sylvia Stout, who, you remember, would not take the garbage out until:

> The garbage reaches across the state,
> From New York to the Golden Gate.
> And there in the garbage she did hate,
> Poor Sarah met an awful fate.

I'll amend the last two lines to read:

> And maybe we should learn that fate
> Before the hour is much too late.

Enchanted Forest While It's Still Enchanted

One lovely day on the cusp between autumn and winter, after the first wind- and rain-storm of the season, a friend took me on one of his favorite hikes in the Applegate, the Enchanted Forest trail. The BLM had kept the decades-old hippie name when they made the trail an official one. It seemed like a hyperbolic name, but Tom promised a beautiful trail.

Enchanted places should have clearly demarcated entrances, so it seemed appropriate to enter the trail through a Forest Service gate into an ordinary oak savannah and beyond that through a second, more subtle, entrance where the hills folded in on themselves, the forest canopy thickened, and the trail started up a dry creek bed bordered with maples. There we entered the real Enchanted Forest. The black arms of the maples lifted a thinning leafy head. A week ago this canopy would have been solidly gold. Now, in this rift between seasons, the gold covered the floor of the dell. Creek bed, rocks, trail, and all surrounding ground were snuggled under a carpet – maybe even a magic carpet in this enchanted forest – of newly fallen, yellow-gold leaves. The thick, twisted, black trunks of the maples drew heavy dark lines against the yellow floor. The slant of the sun intensified the yellow-dappled ceiling and increased the pulsing vibrancy of the moss that covered the rocks of the arroyo and the dark trunks of the maples. When I reached out to touch that moss, my fingers sank wrist-deep into it, like the time last summer when I immersed my fingers into a wolf pelt, the moss as soft and luxurious as the silver fur. Maybe the name of the forest wasn't so hyperbolic after all. I was floating rather than walking through the landscape.

Leaving the maples behind, we turned uphill through the fir forest. "On top of Old Blue," Tom said, "we'll have a good view of both the Applegate and Rogue valleys. Just before the top is a beautiful grove of mountain mahogany, like an orchard in its meditative openness."

As we climbed, the slope on our right began to open, revealing a new road along the mountainside. Bites had been taken out of the forest on either side, like an enraged giant's slashes with pinking shears. Just before the trail turned for its final thrust towards Old Blue, we lost it altogether in a new four-way junction of logging roads. Debris, piled haphazardly over the landscape, lay like scraps of cloth littering a sewing room floor. Tom picked his way over fallen trees, scattered limbs, and bark until he found the trail again. We continued, disheartened but wanting to put the destructive mess behind us and get to the mahogany grove.

We were still stepping over logging debris and stumbling over cat tracks when our trail ended abruptly at a truck tucked into the woods just off a road so new it might have been cut that same day. Nor could I any longer pretend that the chainsaw we had been hearing intermittently all day was from some firewood vendor cutting dead madrones. It was from road-builders, preparing the way for loggers. They were just out of sight, but Tom could tell they were at or near the mahogany grove.

There was no use going any farther, and there was no use pretending we weren't seeing what we were seeing. This was wrack and ruin in the forest. We stood a moment looking at the scene of destruction, at the muddy new road and the strewn limbs and trees, at the truck sitting staunchly in front of us. Then, without discussion, we turned and headed down the mountain.

But before we left, a wicked thought occurred. Tom gestured to the door of the truck, painted with the name of the logging company and its supposed purpose: Reforestation. "I wish I had a black magic marker and a little whiteout," he muttered. "I'd change the 'R' to a 'D.'"

I had never wanted so badly to be a low-level member of the monkey-wrench gang. Not reforestation, but deforestation.

Not an enchanted forest, after all, but a forest like any other in today's world, where, it seems, no magic is strong enough to prevent destruction. The autumn/winter cusp of the day was paralleled by another cusp on which we stood, that of enchantment/disenchantment in our forests. I had entered the trail on one side of that cusp and had come out on the other side.

When Diplomats Dance over the Blood of Innocents

After a long evening stroll through some of the most beautiful parts of old Copenhagen, I sat with my Danish friends Anna and Tuë in a French cafe for a cup of hot chocolate and a piece of carrot cake. While we ate, Anna, just out of college and now working as a political journalist, talked about the Chilean schooner that had docked in Copenhagen the past week. It had been Pinoche's ship for political prisoners. It had been a ship of torture, a ship that had seen men thrown overboard or forced to jump from the mast, a ship whose decks had rolled with blood. Now it was being used as a sailing school, as many tall-masted ships are used in many countries, but its arrival in Copenhagen had caused an uproar of protest. Many people considered it inappropriate for Denmark to host this ship in its harbor. Anna was curious to see it, and so she and Tuë and I continued our walk in the direction of the pier where it was docked.

It wasn't hard to find. Hundreds of lights sparkled from its decks and masts. Elegant couples hung over the railings, milled around the decks, and danced to the seductive rhythms of jazz we could hear from a fancy ballroom deep in the ship. The parking lot alongside the pier was full of Mercedes-Benzes, BMWs, and Volvos. We had stumbled onto a diplomats' party. All the diplomats in Copenhagen and all the dignitaries of state in Denmark, it seemed, were partying on Pinoche's ship.

And yet the ghosts lingered. One could not look at this beautiful ship with its three enormous masts and its sleek design without thinking about what once took place there. One could not watch the ladies in their glittering gowns and the gentlemen in their tuxedoes without feeling the palpable presence of the ghosts hovering about this ship, clinging to its ladders, moaning through its sails. One could not listen to the saxophone and the bass singing their sweet tunes without hearing underneath that music the screams of the tortured, the sobs of the disappeared, and the grim laughter of Pinoche's henchmen.

Earlier that evening there had been a demonstration at the pier in protest of this sort of party on this sort of ship. But that night, when we told our story to Tuë's uncle, who as a young man had been a sailor himself on a Danish schooner, he suggested it wasn't the ship's fault. The ship is simply a vehicle. It has no implicit moral standing. "Why condemn it," he said, "for what people did? Why not let the ship continue with a different kind of life?"

Is Buchenwald a playground for children? Is Auschwitz a night club?

Now that the fate of Pinoche is being debated in international circles, I listen on the news to the protests of family members of the disappeared and to the tales of those who fled Chile in terror, and I think about seeing Pinoche's ship with its vivid ghosts, desolate and silent among the dancing diplomats of the world.

Road Kill

What kind of animal is this in the road, its body shape-lessly mangled and haunches, legs, and midsection a single mass of meat, bones, and still tawny skin? The neck is flattened, the head twisted, angled towards me, ears pricked, nose raised, eyes beseeching, a sweet perfect face, uninjured. Sickened, I pass the car over it without touching it.

Coyote? Fawn?

A tempest of fury consumes me. What difference does it make to identify it? The thing is dead and horribly dead and wrenchingly dead, and it is just as dead whether it is a coyote or a fawn or a dog or whatever, as though if it were the one or the other it would matter more or less. "Oh. Just a fawn." As though to identify it would settle the matter. "Oh, a coyote. Now I know. Now I can forget it."

When I go down the road again, it is still there, but now the head has been severed from the body. Three feet away from the flattened, unrecognizable mass of food for vultures and worms lies this perfect head, the eyes still mutely staring, the stiffened ears still alert, the soft black nose still pointed my way. I stop the car, grit my teeth, and force determination to overcome abhorrence. I find a stick at the side of the road and march towards the head.

The putrid smell twists my stomach. The revolting sight of the severed head makes me gag. The eyes are gone. What I had thought was the stare of death is the hollow emptiness of eye sockets. I swallow down horror and push the head with my stick. It is stiff and bumps with a hollow, leathery sound against the road. Maggots tumble from the neck. A pool of maggots writhes on the pavement where the head has been. I push with my stick to roll the head away, but it isn't a shape to roll easily. Lacking the courage to whack it like a croquet ball, I only extend my time of breathing death. I give the head another push, and still the face lies in the road. I give it yet another and another until finally I get it past the lump of skin and bones it had once belonged to and into the ditch. I fling my stick into the woods, get into my car, and leave.

But still and still and still the rotted smell clings to my nostrils, and when I hold the steering wheel in my hands and turn onto the road, that cloven head with its unblinking eyes stares up at me again.

Walking with the Gods in Delphi

One year, when I went to Sweden to teach at the university in Göteborg and to visit my friends Maren and Lasse, Maren and I took a week's vacation in Greece. During that week we rented a car and drove to Delphi. The sun was hot during our stay, and because it would be even hotter among the stones of Delphi, we wanted to be at the site by the time it opened. By this plan we not only beat the heat but beat the tourists, too. For two hours we wandered alone among the stones, fallen columns, and half-formed walls, once sacred ground to Apollo, the god of the sun and of poetry and music.

In the early-morning stillness hovering about the ruins, the centuries returned. Birds warbled from small olive-green trees like the two doves sent out by Zeus, one to the east and one to the west, that met here, proving Delphi the *omphalos*, the navel of the world. The steep green mountains, carrying the sheen of the morning sun as they had 2600 years ago, made an appropriately dramatic setting for Apollo's battle with the giant serpent, the python. After Apollo's victory his temple was erected, his oracle established, and the Pythian games founded, to be played here every four years. A dark red cliff towered over the stadium at the top of the site, a Grecian-blue sky descended, steep mountains dropped into hidden valleys, a soft breeze stirred the wild grasses around the *omphalos* stone, and with equal elegance to all this natural beauty rose the six remaining tall, graceful, round-stone-upon-round-stone fluted columns of Apollo's temple. These monumental columns holding up no roof, the stone floors of ghostly buildings, the rubble of broken walls, the empty, rounded niches, the solid fittings of polygonally cut stones, the broken pieces of scalloped columns – all suggested not ruins of a culture but its apotheosis, an exultation in the perfect marriage between art and natural beauty.

As Maren and I walked the Sacred Way, the centuries-old path of flat square stones winding through the site, I felt we were walking with the ancient Greeks beside us. We passed the pedestal for a bronze bull from the Corcyraeans, a foundation for nine statues of the gods and heroes of Arcadia, other niches for commemorations of martial victories, and the foundations of the treasuries built by various Greek cities to prove their devotion to Apollo and their status and wealth among the city-states. As I walked, I could hear through the mist of centuries vendors hawking souvenirs of the Pythian games and articles of piety, children whining to skip the worship and get to the stadium, harp music from the theater where the musical competitions were held, and the voice of the priest interpreting the inarticulate mutterings of Pythia, Apollo's oracle, who spoke her divinations from the inner sanctum in a state of ecstasy induced by drinking water of the Kassotis spring, chewing laurel leaves, and breathing vapours gushing out of the chasm of the earth. As I stood on the stone platform of the theater, speaking a silent oration to an imaginary crowd of 5000 people in the 35 tiers of stone seats above me, I sensed the classical symmetry of Greek drama, with its chorus and its epic subject matter, as noble and grand as the surrounding mountains. As I walked down the field of the stadium, I could hear the thud of the discus and the roar of 7000 people crowded into the twelve tiers of stone seats. I could smell the sweat of the athletes and feel the intensity of their prayers before the statues of the gods at the eastern end of the stadium. As I wound my way back through the ruins of Delphi, walking towards the blue sky below me as though towards a sea and facing the steep lines of mountain after mountain dropping earthward, I heard Apollo's oracle speaking to me: "Here are the gods, here in these hills, in these stones, in this beauty. Here, you walk with the gods."

The Ancient *Lur* of Denmark

One summer when I was visiting my friend Kirsten in a little town in the north of Denmark, she was invited to an art opening, to be held at the oldest church in Skørping, built in 1710. "I can borrow an extra bicycle," she said, "so you can go with me if you'd like to." I couldn't think of anything more pleasant and culturally enriching than a bicycle ride through the Danish countryside to see contemporary Danish art and 18th-century Danish architecture.

"Of course, I'd like to go," I said.

We got a late start in the morning, but on bicycles "hurry" is a relative term. We had a lovely ride under a Delft blue sky with warm sunshine between clouds. We raced over rolling country, through a little village, down a hill into a dark wood and over a brook. As I pulled up the other side of the hill into the sun, I could hear, floating across the landscape of green fields, from the distant church with a squat square tower, the clarion notes of what I thought was trumpets. I was afraid we had missed the opening, but it was so beautiful to be speeding on a bicycle through those farms, swinging in a wide curve on the road past horses grazing in a field, so beautiful to hear the horns' distant music as I sped along, that I couldn't be sorry for missing anything.

Kirsten and I left our bicycles behind the stone wall of the church and joined a small group of people enjoying the sunshine in the church yard. We weren't late after all. At the entrance to the little white stone church stood four men, in pairs, clad in white tunics with wide belts and long dark brown cloaks clasped with brass chains and bars across their chests. They held, propped on the ground, long, thin, curved brass instruments.

Kirsten was very excited. "This is so special!" she kept saying. "You rarely see these instruments." They were *lur*, Bronze Age Viking instruments peculiar to the Danes. These were replicas, of course. Only about 30 original *lur* have been found, preserved in the peat bogs. Welded in sections of barely graduating diameters, the instrument curves from the mouthpiece over the shoulder, then behind the neck, to rise high above the head, ending in a flat flared end. It is like a tuba that has dieted into a lithe shadow of its former self. Just as Kirsten and I arrived, the *lur* players hefted the magnificent horns to their lips and played another beautiful extended fanfare in unison and in two-part harmony.

Soon we all entered the church for the opening ceremony. The president of the art association, Teddy Teirup, gave a long funny speech, and the musicians played more *lur* music (surprisingly mellow in the enclosed space) and talked about their instruments. Then, sipping wine and nibbling cookies, the guests walked around the ancient little church to look at the art exhibit: large abstract oil paintings of white and ice-blue Nordic landscapes hanging on the white walls and tiny bronze sculptures, mysteriously elongated, monk-like and dark, on stands around the church.

The whole event was the kind of thing travelers cherish, but as I bicycled back through the countryside that evening, the image I kept recalling was that moment I pulled up the hill on my bicycle, broke into sunshine, and heard, floating across the landscape, the golden, glowing music of the *lur*.

Lickety-Split, Summer Rushes Out

I imagine the year as a circle with winter at the top – hard, brittle, and dark; spring on the right – soft, sparkling, and lucent; summer at the bottom – glossy, bright, capacious; and autumn on the left – fragile, umbral, ominous. The solstices at the top and bottom and equinoxes on either side mark the exact positions of the seasons, like the four points of a compass, but there's no exactness where bright becomes dull or dull becomes dark, just as we can't point to the line in a rainbow where red becomes purple.

That's the image, but that's not how it always is in reality. The other day I was on my deck stripping paint off the windows to prepare them for repainting. It was hot. It was summer. Suddenly I felt a southeasterly wind blow over me, twice, and as sure as if it had been whispered to me in words, I knew autumn had arrived. Summer, in the face of that gentle breeze, turned tail and ran, lickety-split. Autumn poured into the vacuum like a genie into a bottle. As the hot weather gasped its last and dropped dead, clouds and a chill in the air hurried in to cover the corpse.

Once the hot weather gives up the ghost, daylight, too, with its best friend gone, loses strength. Dark, like a huge feral hound, comes in the back door and starts gobbling the light – 20, 30, 60 minutes a day. When I turn around and look, another hound has snuck in the other way to nibble at the morning hours. As the twin hounds of dark munch steadily on, daylight becomes wan and weak, until finally the hounds, replete, lie down and snooze darkly on either side of it, and we have moved into the tenebrous hues at the top of the circle, just before and after the winter solstice.

Well, we're not there yet. We're just here at the exact left side. But already, suddenly, it's too early to go to bed at dark, and once again I have to light the kerosene lamps, now unused for months. Already daylight is deflating like a forgotten birthday balloon, and I feel a precipitous need to hurry. Hurry to get the back yard ready for firewood. Hurry to get the windows painted. Hurry to repair the leak in the wall. Hurry to harvest the grapes before the bear finds them and beats me to it. Hurry. Autumn is my grace, and I must use it before winter sets in. Hurry. It's getting dark. Hurry. It's getting cold. Hurry. Time is running out. Hurry up, please. It's time.

But that's not consistent with the image of the year's circle. Time at the fall equinox is in perfect balance with time on all other parts of the circle. The 24 hours of a day are the same, whether we spend them in dark or in light. "So the darkness shall be light," as Eliot says, "and the stillness the dancing." The year's circle promises that time isn't running out but only shifting into a new perspective. The days stretch before me, promising long, cozy evenings by the fire with a good book to warm my mind, a cup of tea to warm my insides, and a cat to warm my lap.

An Explosion of Stars

In spite of the coffee I had drunk earlier in the afternoon, I went to sleep without much trouble but awoke after only a few hours. The coffee held me awake. It was a starry night.

Some individual stars were pinpoints of brilliance. Others, in my myopic state, were dull gleams. A hard bright shooting star fell to glory with a brief tail just above Humpy Mountain. After a long time another, weaker one whizzed over the peak of the roof of the house. Emerson once said that if the stars only shone once a century, everyone in the world would gaze at them in awe all night long. I think it would be true if they only shone once a year. And yet night after night we have this miracle over our heads, and we glue our eyes to the ground.

Stars are best on winter nights, especially after a rain, when the sharp air clarifies the atmosphere. On this winter night the stars were sharp and steel-bright. But something piqued my myopic curiosity. What could be making that smear of light in the sky in the east? I figured it was two exceptionally bright stars that I couldn't see clearly enough to separate, now blurred together. Maybe I would get up and get the binoculars. But it was warmer under the covers, and this unknown light wasn't going to go away. I snuggled into the blankets and kept watching the stars.

Finally three things roused me: binoculars, thirst, and bladder pressure. I took care of those needs in reverse order and climbed back into bed to focus the binoculars and sweep the sky.

Hard, brilliant specks, both large and small, appeared in my telescoped eye, but nothing fit the murky description of what I thought I should find. I set down the binoculars and looked again. I gave myself precise directions: If I could find that big star just over the ridge and set a line from it at a 50-degree angle,

I should be able to find the fuzzy clump. I lifted the binoculars to my eyes again and followed my directions. First I found the big star, then the line at 50 degrees, and then – an explosion of stars. Never had I seen anything like it. A dozen large blue-brilliant stars swirled in an artist's line of perfection. Scores of tiny jubilant pinpricks of light danced around them. Was I viewing a whole galaxy? Or just a cluster of stars? I supposed it was the latter, but what a cluster! And what unexpected beauty from that blur of light! It must be like that, the difference between life and afterlife, the difference between what we see with our eyes (even with 20-20 eyes) and what we will see when we see with our souls as well: from a blear of indistinguishable light to an explosion of stars.